Folk Tales

and

Fables of

The Gambia

Volume 2

by

Dembo Fanta Bojang

Sukai Mbye Bojang

Educational Services is a printing and publishing company, located in The Gambia.

The moral rights of the authors have been asserted.

First published 2010

Reprinted 2011

ISBN 978-9983-90-108-5

Printed in The Gambia

Introduction

This is the second book in a series of collections of popular legends, folk tales and fables from The Gambia. Senegalese and Gambians are the same people. Thus they share the same tradition and indeed some folk tales and fables. However, the story of Massaneh Ceesay has been narrated and sung by many storytellers and musicians. We felt that we can add another dimension by putting the story on the table. It is a unique Gambian story.

As we continue to be inspired by the great love of our late maternal grandmothers, Fatou Sanneh and Yai Marie Joof, we hope that in writing about those stories that we had enjoyed during our childhood, we will rekindle interest in this invaluable oral tradition. We wish to cover stories from most of the tribes of The Gambia. Thus, the well known griot of Brikama, Dembo Conteh was approached and he ably narrated the stories about Koochi Barama, the two kings make a pact and Massaneh Ceesay. The story of Koochi Barama is common among most of the Gambian tribes.

For the Wollof stories, many of them have been published. Therefore, in this book, we have used only one of the stories of Ya Satou Njie, a native of Ballagharr who now resides in Sinchu Alagie village. She narrated the story about the tug of war which ended the friendship between elephant, hare and hyena.

Alieu Touray, a native of Nioro, Ebou Bah, a native of Baddibu and Modou Jallow of Penyem narrated the other fables in this book. Alieu gave us the story about the treatment meted to the new mother, nanny goat by hyena and hare. We are indeed grateful to all the storytellers.

We are deeply appreciative to Mrs Joanna Mbye who also has a lot of stories to tell. She contributed immensely to reworking the stories in the two volumes of Folk Tales and Fables. Junkung Sulayman Bojang re-read the stories and provided valuable editorial comments to enrich them.

DFB

SMB

Contents

The rivalry between Massaneh Ceesay and Bakary Niuminko

Bakary Manneh locally called Bakary Niuminko was a well known fisherman living in the large commercial fishing village of Bintang in the district of Foni Bintang Karanai. Bakary's family, most of whom were fishermen, originated from the Niumi District of The Gambia. The family migrated to Bintang which could easily be reached through the bolongs (tributaries) by boat from Niumi. Bintang's vast fish resources provided an avenue for expansion of Bakary's family business. Bakary who grew up knowing all the fishing stretches along the bolongs of The Gambia to the island of Joal in Senegal was the secret moving force behind the business. His marketing strategy was tactical. He sold his catches not only in Foni but to neighbouring settlements of Keneba, Kemoto, Tendaba, Balingho and other big trading posts eastwards. As growth was being realised, job openings emerged. Initially Bakary had two moderate sized fishing boats. The fleet increased to five commercial ones. He consequently employed twenty youths of Bintang.

News of the booming fishing industry of Bintang spread throughout the district. Young men hailed from other villages in search for jobs. The workforce grew and the population increased. The money they received was good. Taking care of the needs of their families became assured. The settlement became vibrant.

The impact of growth in the fishing industry and the growing population was tremendous. Food and living needs increased and became more diverse. Business had to respond to these essentials. Bintang had a mild mannered businessman named Massaneh Ceesay. He was a clever man who ran a flourishing shop. There was not an item in everyday human needs that was not available in his stock of goods. He sold the highly demanded items such as laundry soap, cooking oil, sugar, bath soap, clothes, starch, bleach and household items. People from neighbouring villages travelled to Bintang to take care of their needs. His shop, popularly called Massanehya became the commercial nerve centre of Foni. Shopping at Bintang Massanehya was an achievement. It raised the social stature of a shopper.

Bakary Niuminko's fishing business blossomed through hard work. He had no time for leisure. He was determined to become an icon in the fishing industry. He vowed that he would be first and not second to anyone in the commercial arena.

Thus Bintang could boast of being the home of two very successful and powerful businessmen. Fame has always gone with success. Both Massaneh and Bakary enjoyed a lot of recognition which earned them prestige in society. Gradually the seeds of competition got sown although it was healthy. It remained so for some time.

The wealth of both men increased appreciably. They felt comfortable and were able to take time for leisure. It was during this period that Bakary Niuminko decided to pay a short visit to Banjul. He was accompanied by some of his very close friends. There was excitement as it was the first visit for some of them. After preparation for a leisurely short holiday in the city, they left very early one morning. The desire was to reach their destination well before the sun came down. They succeeded.

On arrival, the group of men headed straight to the neat and newly painted compound of their host, one Badou Jeng of Newtown, Banjul who worked as a shopkeeper for the French firm, Maurel & Prom. The gate of the compound was half opened. The visitors could see the clean, well kept yard with its white painted clustered houses.

Badou Jeng, whose house faced the compound's gate, was the first to see the visitors. Pleasantly surprised, he rushed out to meet them. He warmly welcomed his guests and embraced his long time friend, Bakary. He then led them to his house. Badu's wife, dressed in a cotton wax print gown walked in graciously to offer them mugs of fresh water from their water cooler where some bundles of 'sepah' had been left floating. Drinking that water was refreshing. The guests were then taken to their comfortable rooms. They rested.

Bundle of sepah

Dusk eventually entered into early night. A delicious meal of rice porridge with sour milk was served. The company was light and conversational. After the meal, a leisurely walk in the city was considered sensible to aid digestion. The group decided to explore the city by night.

It was a night blessed with the light of a full moon. It was breathtaking. Banjul at night was superb. The sights of magnificent red corrugated roof tops and brightly painted houses standing imposingly against wide leafy orange trees interspersed with guava and mango trees were awesome. The gentle breeze hailing from the surrounding beaches gently pushed the top branches to sway relentlessly. The effect was cooling. One of the guests, overwhelmed by the amazing sight, sighed:

"What splendour! What a blessed city!"

The others could not help but agree. The full moon shone with all its beauty. The visitors, determined to have more of this marvellous atmosphere ventured further towards the beach. It would be a sad miss not to watch the effect of such bright moonlight on the sea. They, therefore, in a relaxed manner picked their way to the seaside.

It must have been a coincidence or divine intervention. At the same time, a group of young maidens were taking a walk towards the beach. They had just been celebrating a 'coming out' ceremony on the successful recovery of their lower lips from 'njam,' the permanent indigo tattoo worn by many young and indeed adult ladies.

The young maidens were desirable. Their attraction could not go unnoticed. Among them, one maiden stood out as exceedingly beautiful. She was dark. Her colour shone like silk under the light of the moon. Her round face was enhanced by a not too flat nose and big round eyes that lit up with every smile. As expected of maidens of her age, she had full firm breasts. Aware of her stunning looks, she walked with grace and spoke softly.

The group could not resist talking to the maidens. Initially they were timid. One of the men, Lamin braved it. He summoned courage and tried to engage the attractive maiden in a conversation. He addressed her:

"My lady, tell me. Why should such a beauty like you be allowed out at this time of the night? You know there are many rascals like me are prowling the streets of this city. I must say that I like your outfit. It suits you very well. May I know your name?"

Flattered by the provocative remark, the lady responded laughingly:

"Don't you see that I'm in a company? You're brave. Not even scared by such a group. Well I'm Fatou. I was born in Banjul. I have lived here all the time. Who are you? I've never seen you before. You must be new here."

Lamin had achieved his goal. He had broken the ice. The lady had reacted positively.

"I'm Lamin Jarju. I'm on a short stay in Banjul with some friends. We're from the big fishing village of Bintang in Foni Bintang Karanai. This is my first visit to here. I'm overwhelmed by the wonderful environment. It is exciting for us to explore the city. With the chance of meeting people like you and your friends, our visit would be memorable. More importantly, we have found out that from here one can travel to Bintang through a bolong within a day."

"I've never travelled beyond the Kombos. I ventured going by foot to a nearby area with some of my friends to attend the naming ceremony of the baby of my favourite cousin. I have never travelled by boat. It could be an exciting adventure," Fatou replied.

"Are you tempting me to extend an invitation to an exploratory boat trip to Bintang? I'm fearful that if I do, it won't be well received. The men folk would deal with me hard for enticing someone's future wife to my village" said Lamin wearing his mischievous smile. His remarks were intended to get information on the lady.

"Ha! You seem to have a secret plan. Come out with it. Are you out to court me for your brother? I'm not betrothed. I'm single. I must know who your candidate is," replied Fatou between laughter.

Satisfied that Fatou's emotions have been set alight, Lamin promised a visit to her home the following evening.

When the friends returned to their host, they made further enquiries about the young lady. People had flattering information on her. Lamin and his friends were impressed. That night they talked of nothing but Fatou. Bakary Niuminko decided to join them at the visit to see the lady. They were convinced that with what was said of her, she could be a good wife.

In the evening of the agreed day, Bakary very carefully prepared himself for the visit to Fatou. He must make an impression. He wore his new dyed dark blue cotton Kaftan which glittered on the dimmest light and brightened his less than light complexion. The trousers of the Kaftan were of ankle length made of the same material. His black leather slippers were specially made from kid leather. They were supple and allowed his four big toes to peep through a narrow slit at the front. The Kaftan hung very well from his broad shouldered athletic body. Although he was not a tall person, Bakary stood out noticeably in any group of friends. In his own way, he caught the eyes of anyone who came by. He was handsome. It was therefore no surprise that Fatou got attracted to him when they met.

At a single glance, Bakary agreed with his friends that Fatou was a pretty girl. He also got attracted instantly when their eyes met. The decision to woo Fatou was his immediate desire and resolve. The visit was thrilling. He sensed that Fatou too had very warm feelings for him. She hanged on his words. She did not resist his move to share the same couch with her. When his hand gently brushed hers on the wooden handle, Fatou did not move away. She seemed to welcome them. She stole glances at him. He returned them with smiles that slightly betrayed discoloured teeth from smoking tobacco. The happiness he felt could not be contained. He had never felt this before. He decided to pursue the relationship.

It was getting late. Bakary, knowing what keeping respectable hours meant to traditional families, signalled to his friends that they should leave. They bade farewell and told Fatou that they would be returning to Bintang the next day. The disappointment showed in her face. She did not expect an early departure. As they were leaving, Bakary lingered behind to whisper to her that he would return to see her within a month. Little did he know what fate had in store for both of them?

Shortly after Bakary's return to Bintang, Massaneh Ceesay decided on a business trip to Banjul with two of his shop assistants in order to restock his shop. Some of the basic goods were running short. More tins of tomato puree, bags of rice, oil, sugar, flour, cartons of milk and many other items were needed. Massaneh, a flourishing shopkeeper was a man who always wanted people around him. Hence news of his business trips was well circulated in the village and neighbourhood. He invariably got requests for free rides on his boat. By the time he was ready to leave, the entourage had grown to ten.

The time of the trip was set for dawn. Early departure with a favourable wind meant early arrival. This would be interesting for first timers to Banjul. The bolong route taken in this trip led Massaneh's boat through the sea front to Banjul. The sights were spectacular. The sea looked serene, glistering under the gentle sunlight. As they approached the tall business houses on the beach front were imposing. They seemed to blend easily with the planned spaces which were indeed the streets. For Massaneh, this was a usual trip. Some of the others were visibly excited.

The group arrived in the early afternoon for the wind was favourable. Massaneh's friends wondered at the teeming crowd along the main commercial street. There was hustle and bustle caused by the considerable business activities. To them that was quite extraordinary. They had never seen so many busy people of various ages at one area at a single moment. They wanted to linger but Massaneh was not encouraging it. He had informed his host of their time of arrival. In the city, punctuality had to be observed.

Massaneh and his friends headed towards the home of their host, Sakou Faal. Sakou Faal was a leading trader of the French firm, Establishment Vezia located at Half Die. He was born and bred in Half Die. Indigenes of this ward were known for their love of good living. To them no expenditure was too high for the comforts of life. They believed in expressing their riches through their women and homes.

Massaneh was welcomed in Sakou's compound. He was housed with his friends in very comfortable rooms with floors covered with nicely designed linoleum, beds quite high draped with white embroidered cotton linens. The aroma of incense filled the rooms. Special well clad attendants were ready at hand to give service.

What hospitality! It was awesome! So all the jokes about Half Die 'poto poto' were just meant for laughs. If Sakou Faal was a sample of the people living in that ward, life with them should be worth living. This was the reaction of Massaneh's friends.

It was keeping with family practice that guests be served with a big dish of delicious Benachin cooked with rice and meat and adorned with a lot of vegetables and hot red Sierra Leone peppers. The aroma and the sight of the food were mouth watering. The traditional drink Sorrel (wonjo) juice with sticks of cloves floating lazily on top was put in rounded nice calabashes with their accompanying spoons locally called 'kork' to drink. The presentation of the food and service was very convivial. The conversation flowed evenly making the meal more enjoyable. The guests enjoyed it.

After eating, the guests retired to their rooms for the customary siesta of an hour. Feeling refreshed after the nap, Massaneh and his friends decided that they would conclude the day with a stroll through the city for some much needed fresh air.

Massaneh in an open locally woven sleeveless beige cotton shirt teamed with casual thigh-length trousers looked very irresistible. His muscular arms conspicuously exposed his masculinity. His brown soft leather sandals especially handmade were adequate for a successful businessman. He was appropriately dressed for a stroll with his friends through the city.

It was common for the residents of the city to sit on wooden benches in front of their compounds in the evenings and watch the world go by. Some of the men folk either played Cards or Draught. Visitors especially those from villages marvel at the difference in customary practice. Yet this distraction did not stop them from greeting people and even volunteering information about their time of arrival in the city, the duration and purpose of their visit. This was a probable move to create an impression.

The visitors wandered towards the southern part of Half Die. The deepest part was at this end, Banjul Wharf. This was a very busy area as most of the ship docked here. Coincidentally, young maidens were heading for the wharf. There were some trawlers that were off loading fish. The maidens were hopeful that they would be able to obtain some jumbo shrimps.

The maidens, Metta, Jorjor and Fatou were engaged in girlish talk and giggles. Hairstyles were examined, admired and criticised. It was at this juncture that the maidens heard the greetings of male voices.

"Good evening. I see that you ladies know the right time of the day to take care of your appetite for sea food. The Harmattan wind is not so strong and the weather is cool. One could wait patiently for the trawlers to arrive," Massaneh uttered in an effort to start a conversation.

"Good evening to you. You are also enjoying the fine weather. Are you here too as visitors wishing to satisfy your appetite for seafood?" Replied the plump dark-skinned maiden called Fatou. She looked up and noticed the clean white teeth of the smiling man who just spoke.

"Yes. My name is Massaneh Ceesay. I'm a trader. I live in Bintang. I'm spending a few days at Sakou Faal's compound. I am here to buy some needed goods for my shop."

"Oh! You are from Bintang too? Some time ago, I met a man called Bakary who said he was from Bintang. Hey, how come that people from Foni like to visit our city. Bakary came and now it's your turn to visit?" Fatou joked.

"Well, with news of all the beautiful girls in the city, should you wonder why bachelors come hoping to win one heart. I'm here eager to accomplish my desire to take one to Bintang. Before telling my name, may I introduce my friends, Mamudu and Lang?" Massaneh asked.

One of the ladies who had a fair complexion and wore a head scarf tilted to the right side of her head took the challenge and said:

"I'm Metta. This is my cousin, Jorjor. The lady in the yellow outfit is Fatou, our creative hairdresser for the day."

Massaneh obviously attracted by Fatou's beauty, lingered as he tried to decide whether to stay and continue the conversation or pay a visit later to the lady that had won his heart. Fatou had won his heart. His friend, Mamudu saw what was happening and came to his rescue.

"Fatou, you'll wonder why we are so drawn to you. When I first saw you, I was struck by your resemblance to my younger sister, Fanta. She's my favourite sibling. You're a carbon copy of her. She's now married and lives in Foni Bondali with her husband, Kebuteh, the celebrated village tailor. With your striking beauty, I'm sure you have done better in marriage by securing the most eligible bachelor in this city. What does your husband do?" Mamudu enquired.

"You'll be surprised. I'm yet to get married. I'm still waiting for Mr. Right who's yet to appear. However, I'm still hopeful. I'll find him one day," joked Fatou. She had become accustomed to being asked the question of her marital status by men.

"Your faith is so strong, I'm sure you'll soon find him. Who knows he might be turning the corner to reach you. This is an interesting discussion. We'll talk more for we're here for the next two to three days. We might even be tempted to come to your home for a visit. Do you mind if we come to your home?" dared Massaneh.

"Oh, I'll be flattered. You are welcomed any time. I live in the compound with the red gate which is directly opposite the Harbour. You can see it from here. Don't be afraid of the colour. You're not in danger when you enter," replied Fatou sporting a smile.

"You are a tease. I assure you I'll not be intimidated. The promise of a chance to see you again is enough force to drive away any timidity," Massaneh stated. He felt on top of the world.

Massaneh was deep in thought on their return journey. He was mesmerised by Fatou's beauty. Although he exercised restraint and did not reveal the depth of his feelings to his friends, they suspected. All his moves to monopolise her attention; the eye-engaging looks and wide smiles whenever Fatou spoke were all amorous signs. He hanged on every word she uttered. Fatou's every move reciprocated those of Massaneh. It was obvious that she was madly in love. Her open invitation to him to call at her home obviously said it all.

Massaneh was so emotionally consumed by his feelings for Fatou that he dreamt of her. In the dream, Fatou was boarding a boat to visit him in Bintang. The boat got caught up in a storm. It got lost. The visit did not happen. Massaneh woke up in the middle of the night sweating profusely despite the cool weather outside, the result of the strong Harmattan wind. The dream had frightened and disturbed him. To him, the meaning of the dream was foreboding. He struggled to get back to sleep. It was towards the early hours of the morning he managed with difficulty to drift back to a light slumber.

Massaneh woke up in the morning feeling very depressed. He was quiet and pensive. Mamudu and Lang observed the mood. They could not help talking about it. They understandably attributed his sad mood to his strong emotions for Fatou. As a very successful businessman, Massaneh had never known rejection or failure in any sphere of life. He had always succeeded in getting the women he desired. Mamudu and Lang speculated that Fatou might not be an easy nut to crack. A major setback was that she knew nothing about him. When Mamudu and Lang could no longer keep quiet about the disquieting behaviour, Lang bravely and in a teasing manner said:

"Massaneh, you are so engrossed with plans to win Fatou since our meeting with her yesterday that you do not care for the company of your friends. Massaneh, why are you so depressed? Fatou is meant for you. She's already fallen for your clean white teeth, enchanting smile and your stunning masculinity. This is obvious"

Massaneh seemed unmoved by the comforting words. He remained silent. He cleared his throat and avoiding the examining eyes of his friends narrated his nightmare. On hearing the story of the dream, Lang and Mamudu did not speak immediately. They exchanged glances before Mamudu offered a weak reassurance:

"The chance meeting of yesterday touched you deeply. You couldn't help thinking about her at bed time. Your doubts and fears on her acceptance of you came out in a dream. Remember this is just a dream. The outcome of this dream could be the opposite of what you fear. Have your chin up and believe that you'll have her. Be the happiest man alive."

"If you're not comfortable with the dream, consult an expert dream interpreter immediately. Any action that would offer relief must be taken." advised Lang.

Massaneh remained silent. The subject was dropped. In the evening, the three friends kept their promise of a visit to Fatou's home. This time, Massaneh was meticulous in his dress. He knew he would meet the girl's parents. He had to impress them. He wore a pair of knee-length well-tailored khaki coloured trousers and top quality white cotton shirt. His brown sandals shone from one hour of polishing. He could have been mistaken for one of the top civil servants working at the Government Secretariat at the Quadrangle in Banjul. He looked much groomed as expected of a man of stature.

Fatou was not only impressed, she melted at the sight of Massaneh. She looked lovingly at him. He was aware what his appearance did. His confidence shot up. He had made a good impression. The girl could not contain herself. She wasted no time to be hospitable. She brought them specially prepared fried fish, boiled black eyed beans and onion sauce. The desert was 'njarr', creamy sour milk shake which was good in washing down food. Although they had already eaten supper at home, they could not disappoint her. The presentation of the dishes encouraged them to partake. The glances they exchanged after the first mouthful raised unspoken questions such as:

How could we resist eating such tasty food? Why should we disappoint her by not eating? Would that not seem ungracious? We must eat. The Creole people have a saying, 'the stomach should be overloaded to bursting point rather than allow food to waste.' The men enjoyed the meal.

The conversation during the meal was light hearted and centred on childhood experiences and relationships with siblings. After two pleasant hours, Massaneh signalled his friends for them to depart. They got up to leave, and to their surprise, Fatou led the visitors to her mother for formal introduction. Although taken aback, the men did not disappoint her. They were able to engage in a very warm conversation with her. Fatou's mother felt comfortable with them which encouraged her to reveal that one of her close relatives, Ndey Maram had married a man, Demba Sanyang from Bintang. She

15

also disclosed that she did visit Bintang once before her marriage to Fatou's father. With duties of a wife and Ndey Maram and Demba's later relocation to Bondali, she lost contact with them. This she has regretted. Fatou's mother was so impressed with the visitors that she offered them an open invitation to call on the house whenever they came to Banjul. Massaneh and his friends were overwhelmed by the warm reception. As they rose to leave, Massaneh dipped his hand into his pocket and gave Yai Abbie a generous cash gift. She was dumb-founded. However, she quickly regained her composure and thanked him profusely. Massaneh secretly felt satisfied. He knew his move had softened a hard ground.

Massaneh and friends on their way back home talked of nothing but of the warmth of the reception and the hospitality of Fatou and her mother. Their opinion was that if Massaneh was serious about winning Fatou's hand in marriage, he would succeed. They then examined sensible moves to take next. Lang came out strongly on consulting a fortune teller for guidance before the formal move of meeting the family to express the desire to marry Fatou. They all knew of Seyfo Bondali Faati, a man renowned for his psychic powers. Massaneh was an acquaintance Bondali's brother who lived in Bwiam. He would be the best person to introduce him to the powerful psychic.

On the third day and what apparently was the final day of the visit to Banjul, Massaneh collected all the goods he had purchased and loaded them in his boat. Early the next morning they left for Bintang. On arrival after an uneventful day, Massaneh unloaded his boat and restocked the shop. With his feelings burning fiercely in him, he left for Bwiam. He arrived late that evening and was warmly received. He confided in Bondali Faati's brother about his desire to meet the brother well known in Foni for his effectiveness in psychic

16

matters. Seeing that Massaneh's needs were urgent, he agreed to go with him immediately. They travelled to Bondali and reached early the next day. Their presence was announced and they were quickly received. The quick, easy access to the skills of the notable Bondali Faati pleased Massaneh. This raised his hopes of a joyful outcome.

With less anxiety, Massaneh narrated his disturbing dream. Bondali listened pensively. He remained quiet and still, staring fixedly into a corner as if under a magic spell. Massaneh and his escort became tense during the period. They sighed with relief when they heard his voice. He addressed Massaneh thus:

"You have a big fight in your hands in your desire to marry the lady. Another man has already shown his intentions to seek her hand in marriage. The response towards his moves encouraged him to believe in the family's acceptance. That man lives in your neighbourhood. He will do everything in his power to stop you from winning the woman. The indications are that your life might be endangered. It will be a battle of might for Fatou."

Exasperated but determined, Massaneh asked:

"Is there anything I can do to avert such a bitter battle that may turn fatal? Could the rival be talked out of aggression and give up the lady? Fatou is the woman I am in love with. She is the lady I want to marry. She's beautiful, respectful and educated. I should not be deprived of the lady with such good qualities. She would be an asset in my business. You will understand why I am almost consumed by the feeling I have for her. Please help me and do everything you can for me to win her."

"It's a challenge but I'll do what I can for you. That means a lot of prayers and offering expensive sacrifices. Your rival is no simple adversary. He is someone with many fortune tellers and Marabouts. He too is determined not to lose Fatou to anyone. The fight will be fierce. The winner would be the man with the greatest substance that secured the superior mystic acts ever known in this area," replied Bondali Faati.

Massaneh was not daunted by what he heard. His determination to marry Fatou overpowered him. He was prepared to do everything in his power to get the lady. He was convinced that Bondali Faati was the only man with superior powers in the region to win the fight for him. His fame of making the impossible possible had been heard well beyond the borders of the whole of Foni. Massaneh needed no persuasion to stay in Bondali village while mystic miracles were being worked out.

He spent two weeks at Faati's home. Sacrifices of a red goat, a black and white sheep and a huge black bull were offered by him. He washed with gallons of magical potions, some of them mixed with the herb, 'timing timingo' produced by Bondali Faati during the praying period. He was given different types of amulets, one of them sewn with animal skin and dotted with cowries. Satisfied that the evil aura that had engulfed him had been cast away and that his body was well fortified, Massaneh was allowed to leave for home first. Then he could proceed to Banjul to ask for the hand of Fatou in marriage. He was on top of the world. With head held high up, he paid Bondali handsomely.

Bundles of Timing Timingo

Cowries

A week seemed too long a wait for Massaneh. However, Lang and Mamudu prevailed on him to heed advice. He adhered. After a

week, they left for Banjul to seek Fatou's consent to marry him. The ground had already been well prepared. The reception which the three men received from Fatou's family clearly demonstrated that agreement to the proposal was assured. Formal declaration had to be made. It was done. Marriage between the two was set. The necessary wedding preparations started.

Massaneh, a non Banjulian according to tradition had to be represented by a native of Banjul. He had entrusted this responsibility to his host, Sakou Faal. Sakou was familiar with all the cultural and legal practices of marriage. The financial provision was impressive. Massaneh felt that as a stalwart in the business field his union with a beauty like Fatou should be fittingly celebrated. Fatou's parents were overwhelmed by the generosity. They were proud that their daughter secured such a match. The merriment seemed unending. Animals were slaughtered daily. Drums beat while food was cooked for the numerous guests.

A month elapsed. Bakary Niuminko and his friends went to Banjul, unaware of the betrothal and eventual marriage of Fatou to another suitor. In the evening, they innocently agreed on a walk to the city. They headed towards Half Die to catch a glimpse of Fatou. As they approached her compound they saw a group of well dressed women sitting in a circle. There was drumming and dancing. A woman, supposedly a guest was going in the direction of the music. The very curious men asked the reason for the celebration. The woman replied:

"You must be visitors. Have you not heard? Massaneh Ceesay, the rich trader in Bintang got married to Fatou today. I'm going to the party at her compound."

What a shock for Bakary Niuminko! Beads of sweat immediately covered his forehead. He started to tremble like a leaf. He wanted to talk but choked. He turned and looked at his friends. It was a sign to retrace their steps. They did not utter a word. It was a painful walk. When they were about two hundred metres away from their host, Badou Jeng's compound, Bakary broke the silence in a stammer.

"I never dreamt that Massaneh Ceesay knew Fatou much more beat me to seeking and winning her hand. Fatou deceived me. When she knew that she couldn't reciprocate my feelings, she shouldn't have encouraged me to make advances. Let's see how this whole marriage affair will play out. A heavy price would be paid."

The words were said in a foreboding tone. They were uttered with much bitterness. Bakary's two friends, Lamin Jarju and Jombo Manneh knew that their friend was deeply hurt. An early departure for home was the solution. Bakary, unhesitant, told his host that he had to leave for Bintang much earlier than planned. Departure was dawn of the next day. Badou was surprised but Jombo explained that their mission had been accomplished. More importantly, there were very pressing matters that had unexpectedly emerged. That night was one of the unhappiest in Bakary's life. He tossed and turned on his bed throughout the night unable to sleep a wink.

At dawn the next day, the three friends quietly left the shores of Banjul for Bintang. Massaneh Ceesay at that time was enjoying his new status, the husband of the most attractive damsel in Banjul. What else could he wish for? He was blessed with a thriving business and more importantly a beautiful wife, the dream of any eligible bachelor. The good luck must be protected. He must return to Bondali Faati to reinforce the mystic powerful cloak that effectively worked out such fortunes. The wife was soon to be handed over formally according to tradition.

Bakary Niuminko in an emotional turmoil did not waste time explaining the reason for his immediate return to Bintang. He was so bitter that he got overpowered with the urge for revenge. He was unable to remain steady anywhere. He criss-crossed the whole of Foni and the neighbouring district of Kiang tasking his old mystic gurus and consulting new ones to ensure that Massaneh's marriage to Fatou would never be consummated. Cost was no issue. What was important was achieving his desire. The woman of his dreams had been snatched into marriage by a man of equal standing. It was a humiliation to him. Therefore both of them must pay a heavy price for dealing such a dishonourable blow at him.

The wait for Fatou was two months. She was then accompanied by her cousins and relatives to board a boat for Bintang. She was finally going over to her husband. On the journey, her boat surprisingly came close to another one. The strange boat was Bakary's. He had heard that Fatou would be travelling to Bintang. Bakary calculated precisely the time Fatou's boat would be in the waters and chose to go fishing. When Fatou's group saw Bakary with his fishing net, they were amused. They must have thought of him as an ordinary fisherman not worthy of marriage to Fatou. Thus came out the mocking greeting of one of them:

"Hi, Bakary. You are doing what no one can beat you in. You are engrossed in fishing eh? We will be honoured if you send some of your catch to us at Massaneh Ceesay's house. We too will demonstrate how grateful we are by paying generously for your precious catch."

The words struck like daggers in Bakary's heart. He was numbed with pain. Losing the woman of his dream to a man of equal stature in every material sense in the same neighbourhood was demeaning.

He felt that the apparent taunts by Fatou's entourage were not only meant to humiliate but also emotionally slaughter him. He couldn't exercise restraint. He called out, his words full with venom:

"Fatou, is that you in the boat? It is your moment to glow with happiness now. Listen to my words, Fatou. Those smiles, I warn you will soon become tears while you are at the peak of your marital bliss. Look, I have a set of a widow's clothes for mourning. They are made for you. You'll wear them soon. I am through a throw giving them to you. Be prepared."

Bakary threw the string drawn bag containing the white widow's clothes across to the boat. It fell at the feet of the bride. This seemed to be a chilling sign that Bakary's psychics had done their work very well.

Bakary throwing the bundle of widow's clothing in the bride's boat

The bridal group was not intimidated by the foreboding threat. They were too immersed in their merriment to take heed. They dismissed the act and words with hilarious laughter. When they arrived in Bintang, they were greeted by drumming and dancing in the bridegroom's home, Ceesay Kunda. The nuptial celebration began early evening and went through into the early hours of the morning as was customary. After a rest of six hours Fatou and the entire bridal entourage embarked on the last leg of the journey to Foni Bondali, home of Bondali Faati.

There was drumming and dancing until they reached their destination. Fatou's group was welcomed in a big way by the family of Bondali Faati. Massaneh Ceesay was on top of the world when he saw his beautiful bride. Griots sang songs of praise of Massaneh and his ancestors. He showered them with lots of money. The merriment continued until late at night when Massaneh had to go to his room with his beautiful waiting bride. They were finally left to retire around midnight.

As is customary, an elder woman had to sleep quite close to the couple on the first night. She would be the first person to know the outcome of the night. Close family members waited outside the bridal room. There was no sign of an elder woman. The bridal bedroom door remained shut. This was extraordinary. Anxiety popped out its head. Surely Massaneh could not be overwhelmed by his love for his beautiful wife to warrant the disregard for customary practice. Bondali Faati worried most. Beads of sweat appeared on his forehead. His patience was wearing thin. He decided to flout rules of decent behaviour. He knocked at the door of the bridal room with all the physical might he could muster. There was no answer. Fatou surprisingly peeped out.

"Where's Massaneh?" stammered Bondali.

"He's still asleep" replied Fatou.

"Wake him up!" ordered Bondali Faati.

With those words Bondali entered the room with force. He saw the motionless body of Massaneh on the bed. He approached the bed cautiously and touched the body. It was cold. He shook it hard calling out his name with a choked voice. There was no response of any kind. He left the room in tears. The axe of vengeance had struck. Bakery Niuminko's threat came to fruition. The widow's gown he made for Fatou would be used.

When Bondali went back to his house, Fatou was with his eldest wife. The two women were not sure of what was wrong. Bondali in his tears and sobs could not explain to them. He sent for his Griot. When he came he told him with difficulty what he suspected. He confessed that in such an emotional situation the bride and the villagers would have to be informed of what had happened to the bridegroom, Massaneh in an appeasing manner. The Griot said that he had a solemn and dignified way to get the message across. He took his musical instrument known as Balanta Balafon, sat in front of the house of the bride and bridegroom and started singing:

"Bintang Bolong daala Massaneh Ceesay

Massaneh Ceesay

Bintang Bolong daala Massaneh Ceesay.

Maanior bey kumboola Massaneh Ceesay

Massaneh Ceesay,

Maanior bay kumboola

Massaneh yeh laa

Bondali Faati la Massaneh yeh laa."

Fatou heard the song and hurriedly rushed to their room.

"Where is my husband?" she wailed. The Griot continued his song.

People ran to Bondali's compound in bewilderment. They were confounded by the news. News travelled so fast that Bakary Niuminko heard of it even before Massaneh was buried. Bakary, satisfied that he had succeeded in his revenge, commented:

"We have seen the end of the story. Let Fatou mourn her husband for the four months and ten days. She will for life pay the price. No man will ever wed that woman. She'll never have the opportunity to play foul with the emotions of a man. She can go back to Banjul."

Fatou painfully mourned the man she deeply loved but more significantly the marriage she never consummated.

Forest residents of Balleh dig a well

Balleh had always known green vegetation and abundant food for humans and animals. The rainfall was generally good for the groundnut, maize and coos crops. The people of the area did not have to dig deep for their wells which provided clean drinking water for them and their domestic animals. They could afford the luxury of one well per household. Good fortune indeed smiled on these people.

There was a long standing tradition which was strictly observed. The community of Balleh organised a big male initiation ceremony every ten years. It was a major attraction which drew people from far and near. The preliminary event was the secret traditional ceremony exclusive to men and boys. The rites were secretly guarded. Women of all ages were deeply engrossed in the preparation of the variety of food and drinks that were served in the entering and coming out ceremonies. The initiated men exuding with pride in their courageous achievement of complete manhood joined the women in the dancing which was accompanied by music and songs throughout the night. The festivities which were laced with the seven day ceremony were extremely grand and merry. There Food and drinks were bountiful. Even the vultures had their share. They boldly descended in their flock on the outskirts of Balleh every night. They had their fill from leftover every night. The waste of food seemed senseless. Little thought was given by people that deep regret could follow because of want and need.

The last seven day ceremony saw the end of excessive excitement in the area for a decade. Famine reared its ugly head in the following year. A period of dry was experienced. Then one night in the first week of the month of May, the area was blessed with water. There was a heavy downpour of rain. Most of the rice fields were flooded and the forest was inundated with water. Water settled even in bedrooms up to ankle length. The people were not initially worried by the early rains as they served as a relief to the searing heat. Unfortunately, the clayey soil did not allow the water to seep into the ground quickly. Water remained stagnant for almost a month. Algae set in and covered the surface of the water. The ground got dirty and slippery.

However as the days passed by, the water started to recede slowly. The people sighed with relief, a sign that they were overcoming their apprehension. Farmers mustered courage and cleared their well-watered fields and planted groundnuts and early coos. But their comfort in relief was short-lived. Disaster fell. A dry spell of three months followed. The ground started to break. The effect became visible. The leaves turned yellow, limp and started to wither and die. The wells too dried up. Cattle, sheep, goat, donkeys and horses grew thirsty, hungry, thin and weak. Some of them got too weak to move far to graze.

The herdsmen had no option but to quietly leave the area with their remaining small number of strong animals in search of more fertile grasslands and forests. The weak animals were abandoned.

The animals in the forest of Balleh although still strong were hungry and very thirsty. They were used to drinking from the troughs that the villagers had built for their domestic animals near their wells. The animals living in the bush became concerned that human beings were fleeing the area. They called up a meeting to discuss what sort of action they should take. The oldest animal in the bush was hare. He presided and opened the meeting thus:

"Friends and neighbours

As you all know, I have been fortunate to have lived the days of yesterday and I'm living in the present. It is a blessing. I'm older than all of you. However, I must admit that I've never seen such difficult times. There's scarcity of all basic needs. I think human beings call our present situation: famine. If human beings who have the capacity to deal with all sorts of difficulties are showing that they could not bear it any longer, what are we waiting for? This area is deserted as most of the people have left. Those who have left have not been replaced. There are no new houses.

We, the animals, as flexible as we are, know that our challenges in life are not as complex as those of human beings. Our needs are minimal: food, water and perhaps the bare minimum of shelter. Now, it seems that we are not only starving but we have no water to drink too. We can't survive without water. Water is the source of life. Therefore we have to come up with a solution to this pressing problem."

"Our elder has spoken. Human beings say that 'the words of the wise are goads.' We should take heed of these words. We have to seriously think of what immediate action to take. I want to believe that we have two options. The first one is to follow the example of the humans and migrate. An alternative to this is to collectively take the responsibility to find water by any means," hyena added.

Elephant pensively replied:

"I have reservations about the first option; migration. Migration will mean that we are going to separate. We stand to lose our much cherished feature of unity. We have lived amicably over the years and maintained very cordial and friendly relationships. I would go further to say that we became kindred. Separating means abandoning these relationships and meeting others with whom we don't share the same chemistry. Living together harmoniously with new animals would not easy. Therefore, I wish to suggest that we look for an area that is congenial in this neighbourhood where we can easily dig a well. Let us avoid areas where the ground is very dry and full of stones. We can all check on likely places for a well. Perhaps some of you have even noticed such places in this vicinity?"

He had seen fox open his mouth thrice to interrupt him. He called up to him:

"Yes, Mr. Fox. Do you have any suggestions?"

"Yes. I think I've noticed a spot which fits your description. There's a place which I frequent when I need a good rest. Do you know the big silk cotton tree which is about fifty metres away from the bolong? People during the days of plenty used to go there to bathe and wash their clothes. Now that place has been abandoned. It's a wet area. We can dig a well there," proposed fox.

"That's a good idea. Who else has spotted a similar area which can be considered?" Hare asked. A pause and then a complete silence followed.

"Since there's no other suggestion, I take it that this is the only proposal. Now, we have to go to work immediately. Let's agree to start digging tomorrow in view of the urgency of the situation.

We can't tolerate the idea of our children being hungry and thirsty. They are helpless, innocent beings. Therefore we are doing this work for the common good. We should all participate. There are no exceptions," continued the elderly hare.

Animals dig a well

Early the next day, all the animals assembled under the silk cotton tree. The wild goat was noticeable absent. They waited for half an hour. There was no appearance of the wild goat. The elderly hare became suspicious. He refrained from sharing his thoughts with anyone. Instead, he proposed that whilst work was progressing, fox should be sent to find out what was wrong. Everyone agreed to the proposal. Fox left immediately. He went looking for goat at his abode. He was not there. He wandered around the area for an hour. He could not find him. He was about to give up when he saw a big shady Netteh tree. I should take a brief rest and go back to the others. As he approached he saw a hairy body from the distance. When he went nearer, he was confounded by the sight. The wild goat was fast asleep under the tree.

"Hello my friend. Wake up! Are you alright? Everybody is at the agreed site. They have started digging the well. You're the only absentee. I was asked to come and find out whether something was seriously wrong with you," explained fox.

"Ah! I'm fine. I decided to take a short nap. You know, I just don't agree with the proposal to dig a well. I'd rather migrate than engage myself in a futile exercise. Can't you see that the whole area is dry? If there was a likely place for a well, the people would have sunk one a long time ago. The idea of digging a well is stupid. I'll not get involved," replied goat.

"Since you felt so strongly about the idea of sinking a well, you should have expressed your views at the meeting. Hare opened the matter for discussion. Remember, it was a family gathering for the exchange of ideas. But you never uttered a word. We made a collective decision. It was never imposed. I'm really disappointed by your behaviour. Now that you have given me a reason for your absence, I won't stay another minute. I'll relay it to the others. I must be going now," said fox as he turned to leave.

When fox returned to the group, he narrated goat's explanation for his absence. A debate followed. Finally the animals resolved that he would not be allowed to use the well when completed. If necessary, they would take turns at guarding it. The wild goat's words hurt them.

The animals comprising hare, hyena, fox, elephant, squirrel, deer, leopard and tiger worked hard daily from dawn to dusk. On the fifth day, they succeeded in hitting water. They were elated. They drank and marvelled at the cool taste. After taking a long rest, they decided that one of them would stay behind to watch the well whilst the others go out in search of food. Hyena volunteered to wait. They would return later with his share of food.

Goat secretly watched the other animals whilst they toiled on the ground. On the day they reached the water, he observed from afar how all the animals proudly shared the first round of water from the well. He looked at them with envy and muttered to himself: I must have my share. He waited until all the other animals left. He slowly inched towards the site singing a song.

"My friends and neighbours of the forest

I'm looking for my little one

He left me five days ago

I've searched high and low

I cry with guilt for my little one

How can I explain my secret to you all?

You'll not believe me."

Hyena strained his ears to listen to the song. He liked the voice and the emotional words. He moved towards the direction he believed it was coming from. He turned to see whether someone was going to the well. There was no one. He could still hear the song but couldn't see the singer. Lonely as he was, he had to engage himself

33

to while away the time. He returned to the well. He then started to sing along. He was feeling sorry for himself for being left on his own for so long. He wanted to overcome this depressing feeling.

He moved slowly towards the source of the music. To his surprise, there was drumming as the singer sang. Hyena was enchanted. He could not control himself. He moved to the rhythm of the music eventually dancing. He danced to exhaustion. It was getting late, yet the other animals had still not returned. Hyena felt tired and decided to lie down under the silk cotton tree to rest. He immediately drifted to sleep.

All this while, the wild goat had his eye on hyena even though he was waiting in his hiding place. As soon as he saw the animal lying still, he put down his Ritti musical instrument and tiptoed towards the well. There was a rusty drum near the well. It was filled to the brim with water. The animals must have filled it up the wild goat thought. He grabbed the rope of the bucket that was lying nearby. He put the bucket in the drum and filled it to capacity. Gently, he took it out and poured the contents into his container. He did not stop at that. He went on to quickly take his bath and left with some water.

The animals returned, gave hyena his share of the food and they all feasted. They had all eaten and needed water to drink. They went towards the well to get some water. They were surprised to find the drum half full. Hyena was tongue tied with embarrassment. With head bowed, he was forced to give an explanation. He talked about the music and his dancing. The other animals were suspicious and annoyed that hyena was tricked. Lion volunteered to take over since hyena's shift was over. He was strong and fierce. The culprit would not escape. He would suffer the wrath of their anger.

Lion took his position near the well. He had decided that the weather was cool enough. Therefore he did not need the shade of tree. He had eaten and drank to his fill. He just had to lie down and coolly wait for the rascal. He did not know that it was going to be a long wait. The wild goat saw the trap. He smiled and vouched to use his trick. He went to his secret spot three hours after all the other animals had left to find out who was guarding the well. He saw lion and decided that he would have to use a different trick.

Lion was used to retiring early at night. Goat decided that he would wait until the whole forest was quiet before going to the well. Lion grew restless as dusk progressed to the early part of the night. After some three hours, he decided it was safe to leave his sentry near the well as the rascal would not visit. He therefore moved behind the silk cotton tree and retired for the night. Goat crept quietly, bathed quickly and got some drinking water for himself.

In the early hours of the morning, lion returned to the well. He was taken aback when he realised that he had fallen victim of the rascal for the water drum was almost empty. The ground too was wet as if somebody had spilled the water. Lion was angry and with fierce growls searched the surrounding. He could not find the culprit who had disappeared.

When the animals came later, they were taken aback by lion's subdued behaviour. He could not explain what had happened. He had suffered a worse fate than hyena that at least had derived joy from the trick that caused them the loss of precious water.

It was elephant who volunteered to take over from lion. He also succumbed to the tricks. Fox, the cunning one took over but he too went the same way as the elephant. Both elephant and fox failed to resist the sweet music. Thus they could not catch the rascal.

On the fifth day, little squirrel volunteered to watch over the well. This caused a lot of laughter among the bigger animals.

"You are too tiny. If we, the big animals did not trap the rogue, how can you, such a 'wee wee' manage to catch him? Don't waste our time insisting that you must be given a chance. This responsibility is much beyond you. The challenge is for big and not tiny animals," they sneered.

Squirrel was persistent. He was determined to have a go at it. With a lot of persuasion, the animals finally gave in. They reluctantly allowed him to take over from fox. They were convinced that he would be of little use.

When all of them left, he went behind the mound of earth that was excavated from the well. He crouched there and patiently waited. Although it seemed like eternity to him, he was convinced that his efforts would be productive. He was relieved when the monotony was rudely broken. He sighed with hope.

There was faint music flowing from a distance. It was followed by a sweet song with some of the words very distinct.

"Kura, Kura Mbissan

You've blown away my sleep

I'm so much in love with you

That's why I'm singing for you

Kura Mbissan

I can't sleep

My feelings for you are as deep as the ocean

Come my sweet

I want to spend this night where the moon is so inviting

In love and true bliss

Come to my bed, Kura."

Squirrel was not captivated. He remained behind the mound. He changed the way he crouched. The music continued for half an hour. He still did not leave the mound. He stayed motionless. The wild goat peeped to see whether there was movement in the vicinity of the well. It was all quiet.

Ha! He laughed loudly. I knew they would ultimately get tired of keeping watch over the well. They thought they could make sustainable decisions. These decisions have turned into ashes. Now that there's not a soul, I'll have a field day. I'll first take a luxurious slow bath so that I can enjoy the coolness of the water. Then I'll fill up my water container to the brim and enjoy a nice moonlight walk back home. He loudly declared.

Goat approached the water-filled drum. He put the small bucket in the drum to fill it up. He then moved some distance away to take his bath. As soon as he had finished, squirrel gathered some sand and dexterously threw it at him. The sand settled deep into his fur and eyes. He struggled to open his eyes a bit. He was surprised that there was nobody in front of him. He turned to look around to see whether it was the wind that blew up the sand. He saw nothing. He went to the drum and got some more water. As soon as he finished cleaning up, more sand like whirlwind flew and covered him from head to feet. Squirrel continued to repeat this trick. This kept goat near the well repeatedly bathing. The wild goat almost finished the water in the drum. Yet squirrel did not emerge.

The animals were concerned about squirrel. They decided that they had to keep an eye on him because of his size. Since he had been left on his own for many hours, they went to check on him. At the time, wild goat had his back to the path that the animals took to the well. He was unaware of their approach. This time he was not so lucky.

Lion was the first to see the wild goat. His anger rose to his eyes. He was annoyed that the stupid goat had succeeded earlier to trick him. He could not restrain himself. He did not want questions and answers. With excessive fierceness, he sprang on goat and tore him to pieces. That night, goat served as dinner for all the carnivorous animals.

Hare, Hyena and the Nanny Goat

One early morning hare decided to go for a long walk. As he was always engaged in taking turns with his partner to take care of their young ones, he hardly had time for leisure. On this particular day, the family had gone out to stay with some friends, just three kilometres away. Such occasions were rare and he was too happy to enjoy the freedom. He therefore headed out of his neighbourhood to spend the leisurely hours in a different atmosphere.

It was a pleasant morning. He just drifted carelessly and without realising it, he skirted past five human settlements. Surprisingly, it seemed that he was heading towards the river with the tall rhun palm trees and thick bushes edging its upper bank. He passed through wooded grasslands and sighted an animal far away. It looked like a full breasted wild nanny goat. As the animal drew near, it was clear that her breasts were so heavy with milk that they reduced the pace of her movement.

Light-spirited hare hailed the wild goat with the greeting:

"A very good morning to you, my friend. I am hare from the forest of Wollom which is not far from here. I got here in my desire to enjoy the rare freedom gained from the absence of my family on a day out with friends. It is a surprise meeting you. You do not look comfortable. Are you in pain? Your walk is sluggish, an unusual pace for a goat known for swiftness," Hare declared to the wild goat.

The goat surprised by the friendliness of the hare, reluctantly responded:

"Good morning too and allow me to welcome you to our small area. It's called Dobbi. You'll see that the dominant tree here is the rhun palm. Hence the area takes its name from it. Please do not be concerned about my health. Two days ago, I delivered a baby. So I'm a new nursing mother. The baby had not been fed the whole day. I had to come out briefly in search of food. I must hurry now because my baby must be crying. My breasts are so full which indicate that she needs me. Good bye and have a nice day." The wild goat turned to leave but was blocked.

"Not so fast," replied hare.

"Why?"

"Can you see that big Netteh tree? It is believed that it's filled with honeycomb. I'm interested in finding out the truth. Let's see who can open up its trunk to get what is inside. I'll go first. See how I do it and then you'll come next. The winner can take all or give some to the loser," proposed hare.

"Agreed. You can go first," replied the wild nanny goat.

Hare stood hundred metres away from the tree. He stood still for some seconds. All of a sudden he started to jump up and down creating a lot of dust impeding visibility. Then with speed he ran towards the tree and instead of hitting it with his head, he whirled round it thrice and fell on the ground.

"Nakam! That was close but I failed to move it. It's your turn," hare told the wild goat.

Nanny goat went to the spot that hare stood to take a good shot. She retraced her competitor's moves. She aimed at the middle of the tree trunk and ran at high speed towards it. Her head went straight to the trunk her horns burying deep into it. She struggled to let loose but could not. She called out to hare for help.

"This was what I wanted. Why should I help you out? I've been dying to get hold of your sweet milk. I'm going to help myself," replied hare chuckling as he went near holding a blue bucket with his right front leg.

Hare placed the bucket some distance away. Then he knelt near the goat and started to suckle her. When he was full he took his bucket and milked her until it was full. He then gathered some grass and placed it near the goat.

Hare breastfeeding from Nanny Goat

"Here is some food. You'll be here for a long time. Take your time and eat it slowly so that it will last you for at least two days," hare advised the exhausted and tearful goat. With that he turned his back and left for home.

Halfway through his return journey, hare decided to take a rest and enjoy some of his prize. He sat under the shade of a leafy thick shrub and poured a cup full of milk. It was delicious. He had his fill. After a short nap, he resumed his journey, stopping briefly at hyena's compound.

"What do you have in that bucket? Where are you from?" asked hyena.

Hare narrated his encounter with the wild nanny goat. He did not mention that he tricked her into believing that he actually ran into the tree. Hyena listened attentively. He had his secret intentions.

"Well, let's taste some of the milk. I'm thirsty," he asked of his friend. Hare allowed him to taste.

"This is sweet," hyena said licking the sides of his mouth. He eyed the bucket which was three-quarters full. He called his wife and five children and asked hare they should all be allowed to taste the milk. Hyena's family quenched their thirst. Just a mouthful was enough to satisfy each of them. The milk was as sweet as honey.

Hare went home with half a bucketful of the milk. He had enough to drink for two days. Then he would return to get some more from the wild nanny goat. He was unaware of his friend, hyena's intentions.

The next morning, hyena followed hare's directions to go out and find this nanny goat. True as his friend described, he found a red eyed depressed goat whose horns were deeply buried into the trunk of the tree. She still had some of the grass given to her by hare.

When the goat heard strange hoof steps, she turned to look for the source of the noise. She was startled with the sight of hyena. She was visibly frightened.

"How are you, nanny goat? You're nervous and fretful. What's the matter?" asked hyena.

"Don't you see I'm in real pain? I cannot get out. I've been here for two days, thanks to the dirty tricks of hare. He got me into this mess. I had a baby just a week ago. I've not suckled her since I got stuck here. If I don't get to her quickly, she'll die. Will you help me get my horns out of this tree?" she pleaded with hyena.

"Oh, my tricky friend, hare. He is always up to some mischief. I'll help you. Don't worry," replied hyena, inching nearer and taking care to conceal his ulterior motive. Hope brought a positive change in attitude in the wild nanny goat towards hyena. She mustered courage and was steady when hyena knelt near her. He held the rope pretending to be untying the knot and at the same time dragging the animal closer to him. He aimed at her full milk-dripping breasts. When they were within reach, he grabbed the right one and put the nipple in his mouth. He sucked the milk. Nanny goat cried with pain as he bit it. By the second suck, the breast was emptied of milk.

Hyena moved to the left breast and put the nipple in his mouth. Once, twice, thrice, the milk was finished. He savoured the taste, licking the sides of his mouth. He felt overloaded with the sweet substance. Sheepishly, he moved away. The goat cried out in despair. She was afraid of the worse. It happened. Hyena abandoned her and left.

Whenever he went out, hyena would pass by hare's abode on his way back home. He would drop in to see him. This day he did not want to see his friend and decided to quietly avoid him. He was not so lucky. His children were playing outside. As soon as they saw him, they ran towards him climbing on his back. Their father heard the familiar way they cried out when his friend ran with one of them on his back. He came out to greet his friend.

"Hey! You didn't tell me you were going out alone today. Were you running away from your responsibilities of care giver? It must be your turn and you escaped. Otherwise, you'll not be alone at this time of early afternoon."

"Wrong! It's not my turn. I had not taken a long walk for some time. I needed the exercise. I went out very early to enjoy the fresh air," hyena explained.

"Ah well. Did you have a pleasant time?"

"Yes. I enjoyed the fresh morning breeze. I'm a bit tired. I must go now. My wife intends to pay a visit to her cousin in the neighbouring bushy area outside Sare Boubou. Good bye." Hyena hurried away quickening his pace.

Hare watched his friend leave. He noticed his discomfort when they were talking. He's hiding something from me. He won't conceal it for long. He's bound to tell me, hare mused.

Hyena spent the rest of his day thinking about the nanny goat. He really liked the taste of the milk. He toyed with the idea of going back when his wife and children had gone on their visit. He wanted another go at her breast. He was in a hurry for them to leave. They departed late afternoon. Hyena left as soon as they were out of sight. This time, he took a longer route via Sukadeboh to Dobbi to avoid a chance meeting with hare.

Hyena arrived at the spot where the desolate nanny goat was still stuck to the tree. Her eyes were closed. She was trying to take a nap. The rustling movement of an animal on the dry leafy ground awoke her. She started, afraid of an attack from a strong habitant of the forest.

"Don't be afraid. It's me, hyena. I won't harm you."

"What do you want this time? You were here this morning. Why are you coming back? Haven't you had enough? Perhaps you want to finish me off this time. I know I'll never see my baby again," the nanny goat said suppressing a sob.

"I will not harm you. Let me have a wee bit of your milk," replied hyena.

"I have messed up the whole spot where I am. It is uncomfortable. Can you move me to a cleaner spot before you suckle? It will be more comfortable."

Hyena was amenable to the proposal. He wanted to be comfortable when having the milk. He went to the rope. As he was in a haste to have the milk, he used his teeth to cut off the rope from the tree. Nanny goat dashed for his newly found freedom. Hyena turned round to satisfy his thirst. There was no goat. His prey was more than hundred metres away. A hot chase followed but the goat already had a head start. Hyena could not keep up with the goat's speed. Nanny goat disappeared to safety.

Exhausted from the chase, hyena laid under a shady cashew tree to rest. Surprisingly he heard these words:

"Good evening hyena. Why are you sleeping here, so far away from home?"

The voice sounded like hare's. Hyena not sure whether what he heard was either a dream or not opened his eyes. He was amazed at the sight of friend, hare standing. He could not help feeling embarrassed.

"My wife and family are away. I was lonely so I decided to go for a walk. I didn't realise that I drifted to sleep whilst resting," hyena replied slightly stammering and refusing to engage the eyes of his friend.

"Since we are both here, I suppose we can go and satisfy our craving of nanny goat's milk," hare proposed to his friend.

Hyena could not believe what he heard. He jumped at the suggestion craftily hiding his joy. They left together quietly. They did not engage in the usual chat. Hare was dumbfounded when they reached the tree. The place was deserted. There was no sight of nanny goat.

"You are surprised and disappointed. I must admit that I owe you an explanation. I was trying to move the nanny goat away from the dirty spot I found her. She seized the opportunity and ran away. She smartly tricked me," hyena explained.

"But what were you doing here?" shocked hare asked.

"I wanted to have more of that sweet milk but that nanny goat had her plans. She deceived me. I did not even have the chance to taste it," explained hyena, visibly uncomfortable.

Hare angrily turned and left. He was very upset with his cheating friend. Hyena aware of hare's feeling had to increase his pace in order to catch up with him. He seemed to regret what he had done but knew it was not a good time to apologise for the whole episode. I was a fool he quietly thought to himself. How could I have trusted her when she pleaded with me to move her to a cleaner and more hygienic spot? The friends were both quiet as they walked the way until they separated to enter their homes. There were no goodbyes. Hare entered his home empty handed. His wife was surprised that there was nothing for the children for the evening.

"There's nothing for the children. Didn't you go out to get us something to eat?" enquired his wife.

Hare narrated how he met hyena in the neighbourhood where he had secured nanny goat. When they went to the tree, she was nowhere to be seen. Hyena confessed why this was so. He had been tricked into setting nanny goat free.

"Since hyena was deceitful I'll have to teach him a fitting lesson. He has cheated us of a dinner tonight. Everybody in this household will have to go to bed on an empty stomach. This should not have happened," pronounced the angry hare.

During the following week, hare busied himself gathering bits of different colours of cloth and making flags. He did not explain even to his wife the purpose. With a dozen completed, he took the road to Sukadeboh. He hanged the flags on the big gmelina trees that lined the route to the city. Mission accomplished, he then went to visit hyena. He had not seen him since the unhappy incident with the nanny goat.

"The silence has been long. It should not be so. Therefore I thought that I'll come and see you after the cooling off period. I was indeed very angry with you. On reflection, I realised that anyone can make a mistake. I've forgiven you," hare said to his friend.

"Thanks for being so forgiving. You know I have this problem of controlling my gluttony. Please forgive me. I did cheat on you," hyena replied.

"Oh, I'm relieved that I've overcome the anger. As part of healing, please join me for a long walk. Will you?" invited hare.

"Yes of course," hyena replied enthusiastically.

Hare led the way. As they walked they caught up with the forest gossip. They had walked for over two kilometres without feeling any tiredness. The reconciliation dominated all other feelings as far as hyena was concerned. They passed some trees and he noticed the flags of different colours at the tree top.

"This is strange. Have you noticed all these flags fluttering on the tree tops? Who put them up?" hyena asked.

"I heard that the king of Sukadeboh is awarding a prize to the one who can bring down the flag that is placed on the top of the eighth gmelina tree, the tallest in the whole area," stated hare.

48

"Where is this tree? What is the prize?" enquired hyena with enthusiasm.

"It's about two hundred metres away. The prize has not been disclosed. Are you interested in the competition? I am," stated hare.

"Well, if you are. Let's go for it then. Perhaps one of us will win."

"That's the tree over there," said hare pointing to one. Its peak was hidden in the sky.

Hyena foolishly raised his head to size up the tree. Greed swept over his heart. He suggested:

"I'll have a first go. I've seen a rope over there. I'll take it and tie it round my waist. Can you help me tie it on the other side and round the tree so that I would be well secured and won't fall down?"

Hare very satisfied that the trap set seemed to work, eagerly helped hyena secure the other end of the rope to the tree. Hyena trusting hare started his climb. He was almost going to reach the top and take the flag when he shouted to his friend:

"Hurray, hurray, I'm the winner........."

The exhilarating pronouncement was swept away by the sudden breaking sound of 'Bam!' The branch he was perched on crashed sending him on the ground as hare loosened the rope which was tied on the tree trunk. On that, hyena lost his balance. He fell and died instantly. Hare's revenge was fatal. It was out of proportion to the sin committed against him.

Koochi Barama and his puzzle

Koochi Barama lived in the town of Sabach. He was the third male child in his family and was lucky to be sent to primary school by his father. Unfortunately for him, his dream of completing his education came to a rude end when his father died prematurely. He could not proceed to secondary school as there was no money for his fees. He therefore had no option but to turn to farming and he spent all his energy on his millet and groundnut farms.

Koochi Barama had a big farm outside the town. He grew groundnuts and millet using horse drawn carts and strange farmers from neighbouring villages. Hard work earned him a successful farming career.

The eligible bachelor was of medium built. He had a charming smile and when he laughed, he showed well-spaced front upper and lower clean white teeth. He combined good looks with a cheerful character. He was always neatly dressed in locally woven cotton shirt and trousers that covered his knees.

Koochi's close friend was the king. During their free time, the two friends played Draught at the palace and discussed their dream wives. At the age of twenty three years, Koochi met a quiet and well-behaved woman named Farma. She was attractive. Her face was round and she wore jet black lip tattoo. When she laughed, the dark tattoo on her gums brought out the whiteness of her teeth. She knew she had good looks and body. She capitalised on it by wearing fitted blouses which revealed her full breasts. Her long loose cotton skirts were tightly tied round her slender waist betraying the broad curved hips as they flowed down to her ankles.

In spite of her beauty and quiet disposition, Koochi Barama's family was not keen about the relationship with the young and pretty widow, Farma. They felt that according to tradition he should look for a young, unmarried woman. His mother, Kumba strongly advised him against marrying Farma. He should abide by tradition. He should not take responsibility of another man's son.

Farma became a widow through early marriage. She was attending primary school when a trader, Matarr approached her family and prematurely asked for her hand.

Her parents, Dodou and Ngoneh were very poor. They virtually struggled to pay her school fees. Hence when a respectable and promising man knocked on their door, they received him with open arms. Dodou reasoned with his wife that Farma's marriage to Matarr would be a quick means of getting out of poverty. They consulted their families on the matter and got their support. They all agreed that parents prayed for good husbands for their daughters. With such a golden opportunity, Farma should be guided to opt for marriage.

The courtship was short. Matarr showed a considerable degree of benevolence towards his future in-laws. He built them a new house of cement bricks. He furnished it with beds in their spacious bedrooms and sitting room with furniture made of mahogany wood. The furniture was smoothly and nicely finished with dark brown polish. The family saw Matarr's gifts as a manifestation of his affection for their daughter who would ultimately become his wife. Thus at the end of the third term, Farma was withdrawn from school.

Aware of the age gap between him and Farma, Matarr tried to get close to her before their wedding. Every evening, dressed in white cotton gown and trousers, he would stroll over with one of his friends to spend at least two hours with her. Farma soon started to look forward to the visits and even got restless when he was late. He always came to her house with cola nuts and black mints which he shared with her family. She would watch him closely as he smoked his pipe puffing the smoke towards the roof on finishing his share of the cola nuts and black mints. Although the cola nuts had discoloured the gaps between his teeth, Farma did not mind. She had tender feelings towards him; in fact she was fond of him. It was when she reached the age of fourteen years that she became the third and youngest wife of Matarr who was fifteen years older. After eighteen months of marriage, Farma bore him a bouncing baby boy. He was named Baka, the first son of his father. Matarr's other wives gave him five daughters.

Besides being a good farmer, Matarr was also an astute manager. He was at his store with Farma taking stock of his groundnut purchases. Farma helped him make the entries in an exercise book. During one of such instances, there seemed to be a discrepancy. Matarr decided to make a random check of the hundred kilogramme bags of groundnuts stacked eight metres high against the outside wall of his store. He did not realise that some of the bags were not well placed and when he bent over to count those on the floor, a stack collapsed on him. He fell flat on his face. He was completely covered by the bags. He cried out for help but no one heard him. He got suffocated.

Farma realised that her husband was away for a long time when she finished with her entries. She called out his name several times but there was no reply. She then rushed into the store and saw the collapsed stack. Frightened, she ran outside and called for help. It was too late. When the bags were removed, the body of her husband laid limp on the ground. He was pronounced dead. The shock was too much for Farma and her co-wives. She was the last to see their husband alive. She could not get over the loss. She cried almost every night throughout the period of mourning.

At the end of the period of mourning, Farma returned to her family home with her five-year old son. There, she worked in the shop which her late husband had opened for her father, Dodou. She took turns with him and her mother, Ngoneh to open fifteen hours a day for business. She kept a note book on the state of their stock and daily sales. It was during one of her afternoon shifts that Koochi Barama entered the shop to buy some bath soap and sugar to find her there.

Although Koochi had heard about Farma, he pretended he did not know her. He therefore started a conversation by observing that he had always found the old man, Dodou there. From that day onwards, Koochi went to the shop for himself to buy food and other household goods instead of sending his youngest brother, Musa as he used to do. Furthermore, he timed his visits in the afternoons to coincide with Farma's shifts. Gradually, he became very close and attracted to Farma. Their relationship developed to an amorous one. People started to gossip about Koochi's long afternoon visits to the shop. His mother, Yama could not resist bringing up the subject one day in these words:

"Most of your friends have got married. I envy my neighbour,

53

Jankeh. Her daughter-in-law is pregnant with child. She'll soon be a grandmother. When will I be one, my son?" She asked coaxingly.

"Very soon, Mother. I'll give you a serious and hardworking daughter-in-law," He smiled secretly.

"Who is she? Do I know her?" She asked suspiciously.

"Her name is Farma, the daughter of the village shopkeeper, Dodou," he replied.

"There are many beautiful young girls in the village. They have never been married. You will be the first man for any of them. Farma is a nice and hardworking woman. She was married before and has a son. I can't see why you want to take up a responsibility of a child so early in your marriage life," she replied avoiding his eyes.

Koochi was hurt.

"I love Farma and enjoy her company. Her son is innocent and I can make him my own. After all, his father died when he was only five years old. He hardly knows him," he said defensively.

"I don't understand why you want to saddle yourself with someone else's child. You should work on having your own," Yama pressed on. Koochi did not like the direction which the conversation was going. He got up with the excuse that he was going to his friend, the king to play the indoor board game known as Draught.

Koochi avoided any further discussion about his relationship with Farma with any member of his family. The lovers were aware of the reservations of some members of their families to their relationship.

They ignored all the gossip. They were both consumed by their intense feelings for each other.

Fifteen months into the courtship, Koochi Barama proposed to Farma. They got married and a month later, she moved into her husband's compound with her son. Living with her mother-in-law and her husband's sisters was not very easy. Their attitude towards Farma and her son was lukewarm. Even if they were engaged in a light and hearty conversation, they would immediately stop when they saw her.

Farma realised that she had quite a challenge in building a congenial relationship with her in-laws. She helped her mother-in-law with the household chores before going to her afternoon shifts at her father's shop. It was difficult to dislike such a considerate daughter-in-law who paid no notice whether her sisters-in-law did any household chores. After some time, Koochi's mother started to mellow down and overcame her reservations towards Farma and her son. She later came to regard her like a daughter.

The couple were married for four years without a child. Their families were troubled. Koochi's mother, Yama was anxious about not having a grandchild. Ngoneh, Farma's mother was also uncomfortable. She spent her money on marabouts who promised that their supernatural powers would make her daughter conceive. Nothing happened for another year. The pressure for a child mounted within the two families. Eventually, Koochi yielded to his family's desire to take another wife. First, though, he decided he had to seek his wife's consent. He so loved his dutiful wife he did not have the heart to hurt her.

"My mother's been asking me about our plans for a family. You know how it is in our society. Everybody expects a couple to have a child during the first year of marriage. What has happened is not your fault. You've got Baka," said Koochi Barama one night when they were in bed.

"I'm aware of the pressure for a child and I don't blame you. Perhaps, you may have a child with another woman. I'll accept a mate just for you to be happy," replied the faithful Farma.

She had some sleepless nights when her eldest sister-in-law joked about looking forward to a namesake from his brother. She knew she was referring to the fact that their marriage was still childless.

"I like Ngenarr, the eldest daughter of the village tailor, Kebba. I've always joked with her that she's going to be my wife. I'll make overtures and see whether she'll be interested," replied Koochi.

Farma's heart missed a beat at the mention of Ngenarr. The latter had completed her primary school education and joined her father at his tailoring shop. She had learnt to sew from him and concentrated on making very nice outfits for women. She was gradually building a trade for herself. Ngenarr was self sufficient, young and pretty. She had the perfect figure eight which the young men of the area wanted in unmarried girls. Her breasts were round, firm and pointed. She had a flat stomach, a small waist and slightly broad hips. Farma felt a bit threatened by the girl who was younger and attractive. Although, Farma had tried hard to maintain her figure, her breasts had lost some of their firmness and her stomach bulged a little under her tight blouses.

Ngenarr was lucky to have completed her primary school education. This did not frighten Farma as she had worked very hard to improve herself by reading any old book and newspaper she came across. On the educational level, she felt she could easily compete with Ngenarr if they had to assist anyone in their community. All the same, she was not comfortable with her husband's proposal but pretended she supported him to consider taking a second wife.

"I'll be happy to have Ngenarr as my mate. She's like a sister to me," Farma assured her husband.

Contented, Koochi drifted to sleep whilst Farma tossed and turned until cockcrow when she drifted into a troubled sleep. She dreamt that her husband had travelled to his uncle's town, Kerr Nderry. He was away for a week without sending a message to her. Then she heard that Koochi was involved in a road accident. She cried out and woke up shivering. Her husband touched her gently and said:

"Wake up, Farma. You're been crying. Are you upset with me?" he asked.

"I had a terrible dream. You went away and had an accident," she explained.

"It's just a dream. May be you are not happy with the decision I made last night. Are you sure you don't mind me taking a second wife?" He enquired.

"Silly! I'm happy with anything that makes you happy. I have a son right now. My womb is sleeping. Go to someone whose own is awake. May be, if she conceives, I will also. It is a belief that a prolific co-wife wakes up the womb of a woman who was taking time to conceive. Wait and see. I may conceive as soon a co-wife is with a child," Thus Farma consoled her husband and herself.

A week later, Koochi went to the village tailor's shop to get a new outfit made. Kebba was not in. Koochi was pleasantly surprised to find Ngenarr alone.

"Ha! I can't believe that my little wife has grown up to work alone in the tailoring shop. Ngenarr, where is Kebba?" He asked.

"My father has gone to Kerr Nderry to buy some thread and trimmings. But I'm here at your service," she smiled.

"I have this material I want your father to sew an outfit for me. I have to attend a wedding ceremony next month at my uncle's compound in Kerr Nderry," he explained showing her the cloth.

"Do you have any style or special cut in mind?" Ngenarr enquired.

"Your father usually chooses for me. He knows my taste," replied Koochi Barama.

"I'll give him the material as soon as he returns. By the way, who is getting married in Kerr Nderry?" Ngenarr asked.

"My first cousin, Ganyi is getting married to the town's beauty queen. Her name is Mbissin. She is the daughter of Chief Habib Touray. I am the best man. Will you come to the wedding if I invite you? Shall I tell your father to let you come?" asked Koochi. He wanted her to accept his invitation.

"I'd like to come and see this beauty queen you are talking about," she replied.

Koochi was elated and promised to convey the invitation through her father. They continued chatting and discussed village social life. He left for home with a light heart. He was inwardly satisfied. He made up his mind to continue talking to the lady. He could not contain the excitement he felt at the thought of Ngenarr. Three days later, he paid an evening visit to Kebba's compound. Kebba and his wife were at home. Koochi was welcomed. They all sat in the sitting room. He spoke to start the conversation on his visit to the shop.

"I came to bring a length of material which I want you to sew into an outfit for me for my cousin's wedding day. I'm the best man and must be supportive to both my uncle and cousin Ganyi," he explained.

"Don't worry. I'll make you an outfit fitting your role," replied Kebba confidently.

"I want to invite Ngenarr to the wedding. She said that she's never visited Kerr Nderry. It will be a good opportunity for her to meet other people of her age group. She'll be able to widen her clientele," he said convincingly.

"Well, if she thinks it's a good idea, I'll allow her. But she's got to stay at my friend, Massireh's house. I'll send a message to him to expect her. She has to be under a protective eye," stated the village tailor.

Koochi Barama was happy. He was making headway in the relationship he was working secretly to change and develop.

The wedding celebration was a huge success for Koochi Barama. Ngenarr attended and although she stayed at Uncle Massireh's compound, she was in his company most of the time. They watched the Zimba masquerade dance together and sat next to each other. At the close of the evening entertainments, Koochi walked her home. Occasionally he would hold her right hand and gently squeeze it. They would linger outside Uncle Massireh's gate looking into each other's eyes. Ngenarr's heart raced whenever Koochi held her hand. She was falling in love. The looks in Koochi's eyes confirmed his burning desire for her. By the end of the celebrations, they felt consumed by their feelings and sweetly surrendered themselves to Cupid.

The love between Ngenarr and Koochi Barama exploded. They openly expressed how they felt. It was society gossip. Koochi's friend, the king could not hold his silence. He mentioned the story to him.

"When is my friend going to tell me about his new love? Everyone is talking about it at the pencha," teased the king, Burr Saloum.

"What do you mean?" asked Koochi.

"You know I'm talking about you. Don't pretend. You've not said anything about Ngenarr. Why are you hiding it from me? Are you afraid I'll tell Farma? She may have heard by now," continued Burr Saloum.

"Okay, okay. Here it is. We were both at my cousin's wedding in Kerr Nderry. The love flame must have been kindled before then but it caught on like wild fire at that time. We danced a lot and very closely. It was heavenly," explained Koochi his eyes burning with love.

"Hum. You must be deeply in love. Your voice changed when you were explaining about this new relationship. Don't wait too long to take her as your wife. Ngenarr is very attractive. A young and handsome bachelor may snatch her away," the king advised.

"Well, I have a king as my best friend. His emissaries to the compound of a future-in-law will be well received. I'll tell my family to get ready to approach Ngenarr's family as my dear friend, the king is in a haste to see me marry a second wife," Koochi joked.

"I'll buy the cola nuts. It is now my turn to stand by your side. I can never forget how you stood by me when it was time to take over from my late father as the king of this area. Let the elders be sent by next Thursday. It's important to talk to your wife, Farma before the elders go. She should be given a good consolation present. She's a dear and hard working wife," he proposed.

"I'm sure she's heard the gossip but we'd earlier discussed the possibility of a co-wife. She didn't reject it. She badly wants me to have a child. She is convinced that another wife might bring children in both marriages. She's such a good woman. I'll talk to her more tonight before the elders are directed on the mission," Koochi Barama promised.

Koochi returned home. He narrated his discussions with the king to his wife. She took the proposal of her husband marrying Ngenarr as a second wife gracefully. She comforted him by saying that she did not need a consolation present. She would welcome Ngenarr as a sister.

Having a co-wife is never a happy occasion but Farma came to terms with it. She got involved in the preparations of her husband's family for the new bride. She was determined not to betray any resentment she had. The wedding was celebrated in a grand style. The king hosted a reception and dance at his palace. Koochi's mother and the rest of his family were very pleased. They were happy that their prayers had been answered at last. Soon there would be nephews, nieces and grand children running around the big compound.

Koochi Barama and Ngenarr were blessed with a daughter a year to their marriage. Three years later, they had a son. Farma too conceived. She later happily had a son too. The compound became very lively with children playfully running and screaming. There was no distinction between the children of the two women. Their father loved them all.

One day, Koochi told his wives that he was going to spend the afternoon with his friend, Burr Saloum. Therefore, he would have lunch at the palace. First though, he would get a haircut before going to play Draught with his friend, the king. He wanted an intricate hair style which he knew would be a source of curiosity to many. The hair was to be shaved with a design. Four patches of hair with inscriptions were to be set in front of the head, a patch on each side of the head. He had secret meanings for the four patches. This was done.

Koochi went straight to his friend's private chambers in the palace after his hair cut. The king was having lunch and invited him. After the meal, one of the servants brought the Draught board. The two friends settled down to play the game observing short breaks in between. It was after the first game which was won by the king that he noticed Koochi's haircut.

The King and Koochi playing Draught

"Hey. My friend thinks he's still a young bachelor. Look at the boyish haircut. This hair style should be worn by your stepson, Baka. What is the name of the haircut? It must be called all for Ngenarr," mocked the king.

"Each of these four patches of hair has a meaning. You can make your guess but the meanings are secret," declared Koochi Barama.

"I'll find out even if you don't tell me," challenged the king.

The friends left the topic at that and continued with the game. The king did not give up. He was resolved to find out from Koochi's second wife, Ngenarr.

Two weeks later, Burr Saloum sent his emissaries to Ngenarr. The message sent was that it had been quite a long time since he saw her. He was therefore conveying his greetings. He gave her a present of Ten Shillings. Ngenarr was grateful. She told the king's emissaries that she would return the visit over the weekend.

As promised, Ngenarr went with her eldest daughter to pay a visit to Burr Saloum at his palace. The king teased on seeing her:

"You are now so busy with the children that you no longer drop by as before when we both played cards with Koochi. Children are our joy. But they can mess with our freedom and time."

"Was that not what your friend wanted? You all kept on talking about children. Now you've got them. Praise Allah and don't complain," she responded playfully.

"I know. I however had been meaning to ask you a question," the king confusedly said unsure of how to address the question.

"Koochi has given me a puzzle. I've been trying to solve it all these days but I've not succeeded. Can you help? What are the meanings of the four patches of hair he has left on his head as designs after his haircut?"

"Your friend likes to tease people with his difficult puzzles. I'll find out for you. But don't tell him that I let the cat out of the bag," warned Ngenarr.

"Thank you very much, Ngenarr. I'll never expose my source," he assured her. The king gave her Twenty five Shillings. She left with her daughter very contented.

Two days later, it was Ngenarr's turn to cook for the whole family and spend the night at her husband's room. Late in the first night in the quietness of the room, she stroke her husband's head passed her fingers through his hair and asked:

"Have you shaved your hair this way to attract me more? What do all these patches of hair at different parts of your head mean?"

"I've had this haircut for some time and you didn't ask. Why do you want to know now?" asked Koochi suspiciously.

"It's just intriguing. I've been studying it and saw some symbols which I can't figure out," Ngenarr replied.

"I know somebody sent you," Koochi observed and reached out to caress her breasts. She quickly and angrily pushed away his hand and turned her back on him. No amount of coaxing would appease her.

Koochi was sure that Burr Saloum must have sought the assistance of his second wife. He was disturbed that the king could get her, his wife to ask him about the puzzle.

The second night, Ngenarr showed no anger. She coaxed her husband into getting the meaning of the hair designs. Although suspicious of his wife's motives but desirous to get rid of her anger, he decided to let her into a part of his secret.

"I know who sent you to find out. I'm not a fool. The person who you're working for has not spent as much as I have since we courted and got married. What has he done for you to go to this length? Anyway, it's your choice if you want to be on his side against your own husband," he said challengingly.

"I'm doing this for myself with a relationship as solid with love as ours. I don't see why my husband should keep secrets from me. No one sent me to find out and I'm not working for anybody," she replied defensively.

"Okay, I'll tell you." Touching each part at turns Koochi explained thus:

"The front part warns having faith on the love or devotion of a step child. Loving a father unstintingly is a virtue of your own son.

The back patch advises a man not to share his inner secrets with a woman, even his beloved wife. You should love a woman dearly, do not trust her unreservedly.

The right side emphasizes that every society must protect their aged and wise men. Their presence is invaluable to existence.

The left part warns that a king has no friend."

Contented, Ngenarr assured her husband that his secret was safe.

The next morning, she waited for her husband to go to his farm and her co-wife Farma to leave for the market. As soon as they departed, Ngenarr quickly got dressed. She disguised herself by throwing a shawl on her head partially covering her face. She then left for the palace to see the king. On arrival she was immediately ushered into the king's chambers. She insisted that she must be alone with him. Her wish was granted. She gave him the meaning of Koochi Barama's puzzle. Burr Saloum was more than pleased. He gave her a present of Fifty Shillings.

Five days later, Koochi went to see his friend, the king. He was surprised to find him in the forecourt with some members of his Council of Advisers. He waited for him to finish his meeting and then they sat down for their noon meal. After resting leisurely in their armchairs for half an hour, one of the king's servants brought the Draught board. They settled down to play the game.

Their conversation drifted to their joyous youthful days when the late king was alive. They talked about their hunting for game in the woods. They enjoyed roasting the hare and any other animal that they shot. Those days were unforgettable. Burr Saloum all of a sudden brought up the subject of the mysterious haircut.

"My friend, I had a very hard time trying to work out the puzzle depicted by your hair cut. No end of teasing you did the trick. You refused to tell me. If I get the answer, you will understand if I sacrifice someone dear to me. You did succeed in drilling the king of this area. the king you call your friend."

"You talk with such confidence. It seems you know the answer. Out with it then," Koochi suspiciously but nervously replied.

Instead of responding, the king concentrated on the game which he was winning. He moved the last seed and then declared:

"A king is not a friend.

Never tell your deepest secrets to a woman, not even your dearest loving wife.

Every society must protect their aged and wise men.

Don't depend on the love or devotion of a step child."

"Now that I've unfolded to you the meaning of the puzzle shown in the design of your hair cut, I'm giving instructions that you'd be killed. Your statement is that a king is not a friend. So be it! Let him be led to the pencha!" the king ordered.

Koochi Barama was led to the pencha where he was to be publicly killed. He was about to climb the steps to the stone where offenders of the throne were killed when a young man came running towards the group asking them to stop. When he reached the pencha, Baka begged:

"My step father is wearing my clothes. I don't want my clothes to be stained with his blood. Undress him and give me my clothes. You can then kill him." This declaration of Baka, Farma's eldest son surprised everyone. This was the child who joined Koochi Barama's household as an infant when he married his mother. Everyone felt that this was betrayal in its worse form.

A man bound Koochi Barama's hands and legs, laid him on the stone. With his sharp knife, he turned towards Koochi Barama. He prepared to deal him a blow on the chest. The executioner stalled at the sight of a grey haired old man struggling with his walking stick. The old man slowly approached the group. He asked in a trembling voice:

"What are you doing with a knife? Who is the man laying on the ground?"

"It's Koochi Barama. His friend the king has given the orders to kill him," responded the executioner.

"What? Koochi Barama. Are you insane? Why should you want to kill such an important man in our community? Let him go. His friend, the king will not forgive you when he reconsiders his decision," he pronounced wisely.

The onlookers enthusiastically supported the old man. They urged the executioner to let Koochi Barama go free. The wise man had spoken, it should be heeded. Koochi's legs and arms were untied. He was led to the palace. On arrival, Koochi did not wait for his friend's reaction. He addressed him thus:

"Burr Saloum, today, you've confirmed my belief. You've also shown that you're not the wise man that people took you for. If you had killed me, you would not have experienced the reality of the meaning of the whole puzzle."

The king was hurt. He concealed his embarrassment in a joke and with a laugh he confessed:

"I was blinded by foolish pride. I felt that as a friend you shouldn't keep any secrets from me. I would have hated myself for the rest of my life if my orders to kill you were carried out. My instructions now are everybody should leave this room except Koochi Barama. I want to be alone with him."

When the two friends were alone, Koochi spoke:

"Burr Saloum, do you remember how we used to share the same bed to sleep, eat the same food from the same dish, play and go hunting together? Did we not behave as brothers of the same parents? You were an only child by your mother but the eldest in the royal family. Your half brothers fought tooth and nail to prevent you from succeeding your late father. Who went to every nook and corner of this area consulting marabouts and fortune tellers to help you take over power? Who went with you late at night to graveyards to offer sacrifices? Please give me honest answers."

"You were always by my side," responded the king his eyes avoiding those of his friend. He lowered his head obviously ashamed of what he had done.

Koochi Barama continued:

"Your action of ordering my death I repeat had lent truth to one of the meanings of the puzzle. I thought you were my friend. You proved that a king has no friend.

When my hands were tied to my feet and I was laid on the ground, my stepson, Baka ran up to the executioner and begged that the clothes I was wearing were his own. They should be removed for he did not want blood stains on them"

The king was amazed. He asked loudly:

"What? You mean the boy you cared for as your own? Farma's son with her late husband did that? I can't believe what I'm hearing. You went against your family's wish and married a widow who had a child. And that child gave nothing back but betrayal."

"Yes. Baka, the boy whom I said was my eldest son. He proved that one cannot depend on the love of a step child," replied Koochi Barama.

"Just before the man struck me with the knife, an old man walked slowly towards us and enquired what was happening. When he was told that you had ordered my killing, he stopped the executioner from carrying out the instructions. He warned that the king might relent and regret giving the order. He reasoned that I was an important man in our society. Did this not show the value of having elderly wise men in any community?" Koochi Barama asked.

"This is amazing. I never thought that all these scenes could have unfolded as a result of my orders," the king wondered loudly.

"Finally, I must say I made the mistake of confiding in my wife, Ngenarr. I told her the secret which she promised to keep. She failed me. She did not give due consideration to how much I've done for her during both our courtship and marriage. She was easily carried away by the presents you gave her. I'm quite sure you gave her amounts of money that overwhelmed her." Koochi Barama concluded.

Burr Saloum was silent, regretful of the treatment he gave to a loyal friend.

Hare gets Hyena and Elephant to work on his farm

There were two friends living in the forest of Sare Bundu. They were fondly called Maubeh Hyena and Maubeh Hare by their friends. The two would spend hours talking a lot with admiration about the ways of life of human beings. They marvelled at the system of government and their various means of earning a living. Farming was especially attractive to them. One day, in the course of such chats, they agreed to experiment on farming by sharing one.

Maubeh Hyena and Maubeh Hare both went out to look for a suitable area for their farm. They came across a patch of dry grassy land in the neighbourhood of Sare Alpha. It was about one hectare in size. It would not take a lot of time in preparing it for farming because there was very little grass on the ground. On looking at the soil, they decided that the best crop that would give a good yield would be millet. Since the rains had started to fall, they should immediately clear the land.

Whilst they were planning, Maubeh Hare's mind was engaged on other things. He looked at the area and mused:

Sweating under this sweltering sun to clear this land would be tough for me. Someone else would have to do it for me. I must go to my friend, the elephant and talk to him sweetly. He may oblige. Maubeh Hyena and Maubeh Hare had agreed to start clearing the new farm in two days time. That was good enough time for Maubeh Hare to visit elephant. The next day, he wasted no time to go in search of his friend. He was lucky. He met him with his wife in an amorous mood under the shade of the fast growing evergreen neem tree.

"My dear friend, it seems I'm disturbing you at a very intimate moment," hare said hiding a smile.

"Well, my dear little Maubeh is good at disturbing me when I'm in an amorous mood. This is not the first time," replied elephant jokingly.

"Oh, really? Well I'm sorry. I dreamt of you last night and since I've not seen you for a long time, I decided that I must see you this morning to check that you're in good health," explained Maubeh Hare.

"That's very thoughtful of you. You're so kind but I'm feeling good as you can see even though today has been too humid. Perhaps, it will rain later," elephant replied.

"Well, you know what this area is like during the rainy season. The temperature can be intolerable. What are your plans this year?"

"I've not thought about anything yet. What about you?"

Maubeh Hare hesitated, cleared his throat and then explained:

"I've been playing with the idea of growing millet on a plot of land that I've seen in Sare Alpha. I thought of offering the opportunity to co-share with me, if you're interested. It is a good way to provide food for your family. If you are well stocked in food, you'll be independent."

He was anxious about the kind of answer the elephant would give. His friend was too heavy to welcome toiling under the hot burning sun. To Maubeh Hare's relief, the elephant said:

"This is a good idea. It could also be interesting. I'll spend my time doing some useful work which can earn me more food. The amount of food I need a day for my family is more than ten times that of yours. If I work hard I will produce enough and even keep some for those dry days when food would be difficult to come by. But the division of our yield should be fair. It should be proportional to the amount of work done by each."

The idea of sharing did not please Maubeh Hare. He replied:

"The farm is mine and I came up with the idea. Therefore, my share would be sixty percent. You should be happy with forty percent."

"Make it fifty-five percent for yourself and forty-five for me. My needs are more than yours. I eat more than you do. I'm heavier. Yet you expect me to work as long and as much as you do," countered elephant.

"All right. I won't quarrel with you over this. I gladly accept your proposal. Let's go so that I'll show you the plot. We will observe this work plan. For the first two days, you'll work in the afternoons and I'll do the mornings. Then we'll exchange shifts," explained hare.

"It is agreed. Let's go now. I want to see the area you're talking about."

The two friends departed and because of elephant's slow pace, the journey lasted longer than it should have taken. They arrived at the place and Maubeh Hare pointed out the area of the farm.

"This is the plot of land we should cultivate. It starts on this wooden post here. I have already demarcated its four corners with these wooden posts," explained Maubeh Hare.

"I can see that. This land is big. What's the size?"

"It's just one hectare. Surely that's not big."

"You're joking. That's not 'just.' If it wasn't big, why did you take the trouble to enlist my help? With such a size, we'll have to review how we share our produce," elephant stated provokingly, looking directly into hare's eyes.

"All right. However, let's not count our chickens before they are hatched. We'll carefully examine the division of the harvest when the crop is ready. Meanwhile let us start to do the essential work as soon as we can. How about beginning tomorrow?"

Elephant agreed to the proposal. Hare gave him a hoe, the implement needed for weeding. Then they bade each other farewell and went their separate ways. When elephant returned to his wife, he narrated Maubeh Hare's proposal to her. She listened attentively and then commented:

"It seems Maubeh Hare never responded to the issue of revisiting the way of sharing the crop yields. You should have committed him to a firm agreement. The easy way you let him go makes room for cheating."

"I know. He's my friend and as I thought of his gesture as kind I found it difficult to push too hard. I saw the partnership in the farm as a means to guarantee food for the family in times of scarcity," replied elephant secretly wishing he was firmer with hare as advised by his wife.

Early the next day, it was Maubeh Hyena who left his abode for the farm with a hoe hanging half way round his neck. He had the morning shift as agreed with Maubeh Hare. He passed by hare's place to tell him that he would leave the farm a little after midday, the end of his shift.

At the farm, hyena regarded the palm wine tree in the middle as the spot where he wanted to stop on the first day of clearing the farm of weeds. He started from one corner of the wooden post and worked towards the tree. The sky was overcast and thick clouds covered the sun as if it was going to rain. With this tempered weather he was able to dig out some of the deeply rooted stubborn Bankanas (Wollof) shrubs. By midday, he was exhausted by such intensive work. As soon as he reached the targeted spot under the tree, he put down the hoe. He stood under the shade for some time. He was sweating and breathless. He decided that he must take a rest. He needed to regain his composure. When he had cooled off he decided it was time to go home.

Hyena under the tree

It was about that time that elephant bade farewell to his wife and family. He wanted to get to the farm before the sun reached directly overhead. He succeeded and arrived some few minutes after hyena's departure. He inspected the work that had been done and wondered:

I can't believe that small animal; Maubeh Hare could clear all this area alone. He does not have the strength to even use a hoe to remove the grass much more uproot the Bankanas shrubs. That's no mean feat. Someone must have helped him. No matter how he did it, I'll show him that I can do better.

With fervour, elephant started to weed with his hoe. His weight was an impediment. He got tired very easily but defied the urge to lay down his hoe. He persevered. From time to time, he would pause a little and then resume as soon as he regained his breath. By the time that the sun was fading in the horizon, he was able to remove all the grass from the end of one of the wooden post to the other side of the palm tree where hyena had stopped. He was pleased with his achievement. He said to himself that his friend, hare would see that he was no match. Towards dusk, he left the farm for home.

At night, hare went for a walk. He was curious to know how far elephant and hyena had got in the weeding of the farm. On arrival, he was amazed. He looked at the two different patches of land obviously cleared by his two friends. He smiled cunningly.

"They'll do all the work and I'll reap the benefits. Me, I won't even touch a hoe," he muttered.

Hyena and elephant were able to clear the farm within three days. A day before they finished clearing, Maubeh Hare visited each of them. He gave them some millet seeds to sow on the farm. They were both ignorant of each other's toil in the farm although they innocently competed over performance on their daily output in the farm. They were also unaware that hare was cheating on them. They worked whilst hare slept and idle away in a quiet corner.

As the rains were good the shoots of the millet soon began to blossom. The leaves were green and healthy. The stalks towered with heads of grains sticking out. The farm caught the eyes of passersby. Everyone talked of the promises of a bumper harvest. Maubeh Hare heard the rumours so he went to visit elephant.

"It's been a long time since we saw each other. Work on the farm has taken up all our time. How are you?" he asked his friend.

"It's good you're here. I've been thinking of paying you a visit. You know that during our discussion the last time we never reached a decision on how to divide the yields of the farm. It is now time to agree since the crop has blossomed," replied elephant.

"Indeed. I'm open to your suggestion. But first, let me explain to you what brought me here."

"I will listen. You always have news about other animals in the forest. What's the latest?" questioned elephant.

"You want to hear the latest gossip in the forest, eh? On my way here I accidentally came across a friend, the bush fowl. He said that hyena confided in him that he, Maubeh Hyena plans to secretly go to our farm and help himself with our millet crop," whispered hare.

Elephant was enraged.

"After toiling so hard, someone else intends to come, rob us of our crops and enjoy the fruits of our labour. I won't sit by and see hyena do that. Where is he?" he pronounced his voice trembling with emotion.

"His plans are to go there alone on Wednesday night that is, in two days' time," explained hare.

"Let's see whether there'll be an opportunity for him to carry out his scheme," threatened elephant.

Hare bade farewell to elephant after agreeing to meet on Wednesday evening at the farm. Treacherously he went straight to see Maubeh Hyena.

"My friend, I see that you have more time to yourself. You've been resting but you have also been watching the millet blossom. Very soon we'll start harvesting what we've worked so hard to produce. We can look forward to enjoying the fruits of our labour."

"Yes, yes, indeed. I can't wait to get over with the harvesting. It's obvious that it was worth the energy spent, you know," replied hyena with satisfaction.

"I know. The only snag is, I've just heard of an interesting rumour. You know everybody has been talking about our farm. Elephant is jealous. He intends to go to the farm late at night to harvest it secretly."

"When does he plan to do that?" asked hyena suspicious but also angry.

"I don't know how true it is. But I understand he says Wednesday night," hare revealed.

"I'll prevent him from his mischievous act. I'll be there. Make sure you come too," stated hyena.

On the agreed day, hare met elephant at the farm. They looked for a place to hide. The plan was not to be seen. They chose the cashew tree. It was big and leafy. It could adequately conceal elephant. The big animal climbed the tree leaving his big bag which was to contain his share of the harvested crop on the ground. Since he was heavy, hare advised him that for safety reasons, he should be bound on to the strong branch he was sitting on. Elephant thought it a good idea and innocently agreed. Hare lied to him that he was going to hide too so that together they could launch a surprise attack on hyena as he entered the farm.

Elephant bound up the tree

Maubeh Hare had a different plan. He did not hide as he told elephant but rushed to Maubeh Hyena as he entered the farm. Maubeh Hare whispered to him:

"I just saw elephant. He's boasting with confidence that he would devour all the crops in the farm. He is challenging any of us to stop him."

"That big and lazy fool! Is he threatening us? I'll teach him a lesson. Where is he?"

"He's on his way to the farm, I'm sure. If you leave now, you'll definitely meet him there," replied hare.

"All right. Let's go."

Maubeh Hyena and Maubeh Hare hurried to the farm. On arrival, Maubeh Hare pretended to see for the first time something strange dangling from the cashew tree. He went nearer. He saw a bag at the foot of the same tree. He appeared as if frightened.

"Hare, what is that dangling on the cashew tree? There is something lying at the foot of the tree also? Is lion hiding there? This cannot be elephant. The creature seems to be more than elephant," Hyena asked as he turned on his heels with speed. He fled.

Hare could not contain himself. He collapsed with laughter. Hyena's reaction was too funny to see.

"Get me down," elephant commanded his friend, Maubeh Hare.

"Are you talking to me? I will not. Do you want me to help you get down? You must be dreaming. Enjoy the night on the leafy branch. Good bye," replied hare.

Elephant shocked at what he heard, resigned himself to his fate. He dangled until he fell off the branch. He died.

The next morning, Maubeh Hare returned to the farm to find elephant dead. Birds and vultures were having a feast. He stood for a long time and then said: "Yes. I'm now alone. All this millet is mine!"

Hyena, Hare and Elephant register
for a tug of war contest

At the end of each trade season, the people of Sanjal under the leadership of their chief Barham Sabally would organise different activities as entertainment. People came from Baddibu, Ballangharr and Saloum to attend the masquerade dance, wrestling and the game of draught among other amusements. This particular year, Chief Barham Sabally consulted his advisers with a view to introducing a new contest. They decided that a tug of war or test of physical might would be a good amusement for not only the people of Sanjal but the participating neighbouring areas too. The events were well publicised. Kumba Sabally, the Chief's eldest sister known for her jovial nature and one Morr Cessay were given the responsibility of publicity. Morr Ceesay was regarded by everyone as the most talkative person ever known. Kumba Sabally was a good choice. The adage that 'all succeeds with people who are sweet and cheerful' could only be realised with her involvement. The two of them were able to arouse interest among the people of the whole area. Even the animals living in the neighbourhood got engaged in the talk of the events. Kumba Sabally and Morr Ceesay had indeed done their work very well.

Elephant, hyena and hare lived in the thick grassland area outside Ballangharr. They decided to be part of the competition and chose the tug of war. They knew that each of them would have to be transformed to human beings in order to be eligible. They went to the chief's compound to register their interest. The three changed into young men in their early thirties. They sought audience with the chief.

"Salamu alaikum,

I'm Ali Saine. I come from the village of Sorchu. I am here to say that I want to take part in the competition which you are organising this year," said the fattest of the three men. It was the elephant who had become a human being.

"Welcome to Sanjal. We are more than happy to include our neighbours in our social activities. The white man says that 'all work and no play will make Jack a dull boy.' My people are capable of working hard but then they believe in entertaining themselves afterwards. This has become a normal event in our lives for some time now. I'm pleased that our neighbours have been responding to our invitations. This year, I want to introduce other forms of entertainment. A tug of war will be organised. There'll be an attractive prize. The winner would get a reward which is a secret," explained Chief Barham Sabally.

"We heard about this competition. I'm also interested in taking part. I'm from Dangall," stated Beran Gaye, the man with the athletic body. This was hare that had changed into a handsome, medium built light skinned man.

"Let me now introduce myself, sir. My name is Katim Njie. I live in Helou. I too want to register my interest in the competition," explained the tall and lanky Katim Njie. He smiled begrudgingly. He had lost his two front teeth. He strenuously avoided laughing. Katim was no other but the hyena that changed into a man.

"I'm delighted to hear that you are interested in taking part in the competition. Hassoum, kindly take note of these young men. Take them round. Show them the rope that would be used so that they'll have a feel of it. Also take them to the arena where the competition would be held," directed the chief.

The three visitors followed Hassoum. They were shown the long, thick rope that would be in use. He also took them to the arena which was a wide sandy place thirty metres by forty metres in length and breadth. Some gmelina trees covering the perimeter served as the fence with the numerous branches giving shade to the arena. They studied the ground before bidding farewell to Hassoum. They promised to be back for the contest.

As soon as the three friends reached the forest, they went back to their natural forms. They were excited about the event and discussed what they would do.

"I wonder why the prize of the contest is shrouded in secrecy. Perhaps, it's a sheep," hare said to start the conversation.

"It may be a bull," said the elephant.

"For all you know, it can be a cock," joined in the hyena.

"Let's not waste time with guessing. We have only two full days before the event. As close friends, we should not allow the prize to get into the hands of other competitors. Let's decide what to do in order to win. Also, if any of us wins, the other two who did not should be catered for," proposed hare.

"What are you trying to say? The winner should be given special treatment" queried hyena.

"I think we should first try to establish who would be the best amongst us in the game of tug of war. Then we can talk about winning and sharing the prize," stated hare.

"Well, to know the best, let's put it to the test. Bring a rope. You and I will start. Then you'll draw with hyena. The last contest will then be between hyena and I," elephant spoke up.

"You know I'm a single parent. I've got to find food for my little ones very early in the morning. Thus I can't function until in the evening. The two of you can hold your contest in the morning. My turn should be arranged for late afternoon," explained hare.

"Okay. I suppose we should be more reasonable with you. You have your morning responsibilities. Tomorrow, hyena and I will start. You'll take me on in the evening. Let's go so that you can give us the rope" agreed elephant.

Hyena, elephant and hare discussing the tug of war contest

They departed for hare's living area. They got the rope from him. They also searched for a suitable place to hold their contests. An empty space between a mango and cashew tree was found and selected. The size was good. It was on the outskirts of **Sorchu.**

The next morning, hyena and elephant met at the agreed location for their contest in the morning. Both of them got there on time. Each chose where to stand and held an edge of the rope. Hyena stood near the cashew tree and passed the rope round his waist. Both arms were to be engaged in the pulling. Elephant opted to take his position near the mango tree and wound the rope five times round his trunk. After counting three, they started to pull. They were both determined to win. Hyena pulled towards himself whilst elephant tugged with his trunk. The rope was made of nylon so it was too slippery. It slid across hyena's waist and he fell heavily on his back. His waist was bruised and his back ached. He could not get up. He swore under his breath as he rolled on his side to steal a look at his opponent. Elephant was standing with his gaze fixed on the ground. Hyena could not see what had engaged elephant's attention.

"Well, you've won. Can you come and give me a hand. I can't move. My back aches," screamed hyena.

"It's not that I don't want to help you. I can't. I've hurt my trunk and it's bleeding," trumpeted elephant.

"What! Hare should pay for this. He knew that his rope was no good," threatened hyena.

The two animals became suspicious that hare had tricked them. Hare was mischievous. They could not understand why hare suggested that they compete against each other. This made hyena go out and look for hare. Hyena saw hare. In pretence he asked:

"Where is elephant? I've missed him. Although you gave us the rope, he didn't appear for our contest. I am sure you have another rope. If so, the two of us can start our contest. The sun will soon set."

"I saw elephant go past here. He didn't see me though. That big cashew tree must have hidden me from him," replied hare.

"Well, since he's gone, I suppose we can start our own contest. The big prize may be my catch," pressed hyena.

Hare was not prepared for a contest just then. Besides, he was yet to find out what had happened between his two friends.

"You know, I'm just from a long search for my youngest leveret. When I returned home around midday with food for my leverets, the youngest was absent. On enquiring, I was told that she was playing outside. But she wasn't there. I roamed through the whole area but couldn't find her. Discouraged, I decided to return home. On my way I saw a sleeping figure under a neem tree. I went close and there she was fast asleep. What a relief for me! Now that I've just arrived, I need some rest. I do know I wanted my contests in the evenings but you will agree that it would be very unfair if you insist that I compete right now. It was agreed that elephant, you and I would hold the contest at the area's meeting centre in two days time. But this must change. You know the proverb that 'children are the reward of life.' I couldn't rest until I found my baby. Searching for her has really sapped my energy as such I'm unable to do anything now. Can we please do it tomorrow? I'll come for you as soon as I complete my duties to my little ones," hare pleaded, stretching out his forearms, groaning to emphasize his fatigue.

"Okay, I can't quarrel with your reasoning. It's tomorrow then. Both contests will be held," agreed hyena.

If he thinks he can fool me, he's making a big mistake. I'll not engage in a physical show of strength with him until I know what happened between him and elephant, hare mused.

Early in the evening, elephant went out looking for hare. He met him at the end of the forest between the villages of Sorchu and Dangall. He did not know that hyena had already tried to engage hare in the competition but failed.

"Well my friend. I suppose you're well prepared for our competition. How're your little ones?" enquired elephant.

Hare narrated the same story which he told hyena about how his youngest leveret went missing. Elephant listened sympathetically. He avoided looking at hare on the face for fear he would notice his wounded trunk. Unfortunately, hare was unsteady. He kept moving round so that he could stand directly in front of elephant. He suspected that his friend was hiding something from him.

"What's wrong? You don't seem yourself," enquired hare.

"Oh, I'm fine. Have you seen hyena?"

"What were you doing? What is this wound on your trunk?" hare asked secretly suppressing his amusement.

"I, I was clawed by a hare," stammered elephant.

"Impossible! How can that happen?

"You want to know? Let's bring out your eldest leveret. We'll soon see how it happened," trumpeted elephant. At this moment hyena appeared.

"Hello, my dear hyena! How are you?" shouted hare deliberately ignoring elephant's proposal.

"Hi! My friends! Are you getting ready for the contest?" hyena called out.

"Oh, I was just narrating to elephant how I almost lost my mind because my baby decided to give me a rough time. She was with her siblings but then disappeared. I searched everywhere for her. I almost gave up when I saw her sleeping under a neem tree. This child's sudden disappearance almost gave me a heart attack," explained hare.

"Elephant, I thought I'll find you in the outskirts of **Sorchu.** Tell me, is this competition between the two of you going to take place?" asked hyena cunningly.

"Hyena, you're walking in a strange way. Are you in great pain? You're hardly using your forefeet," asked hare changing the subject of their conversation as it touched her.

"I was clawed by a hare," explained hyena.

"Both of you sustained injuries? Impossible! How can that happen?" asked hare.

"Come with us. We'll show you how it happened," replied elephant.

Elephant wandered towards the direction of Dangall, closely followed by hare and hyena. They reached the mango tree where elephant had stood earlier for the tug of war against hyena. Elephant went behind to get the rope. Hyena sprang and as hare tried to run, he seized him by the neck and dragged him. Elephant quickly threw the rope to him. He got it round the neck, drew it tightly and bound the forefeet of hare. The other edge was tightly fastened round the tree trunk.

"Ha! You thought you were smart and fast. This time around your tricks won't work. How about testing whether you are as cunning as a fox under this shady tree? Hare, you can have a nice rest," jeered hyena.

Elephant and hyena turned and left their friend behind. They were satisfied that they had got back at him. He had tricked them into a tug of war which had brought them a lot of pain and discomfort. It was his time to have his share of the same.

Hare tried to untie the rope but his efforts were unsuccessful. Exhausted he laid on the ground aggressively turning and twisting until his whole body became reddish brown because of blood covered bruises. Limply he leaned against the tree pretending to be asleep. Towards nightfall, elephant and hyena went to check on their friend. They wanted him to spend the night there as a punishment.

They approached and saw their friend in a miserable state. They could hear him crying as they got nearer. There were tears in his eyes. His whole body was as red as blood. He appeared as if he was fiercely attacked. He was a pitiful sight.

"Please let me go. They almost killed me," begged hare.

Hyena was sorry for him. He went to the tree and loosened the rope from the trunk. Hare leaped and rushed in the direction of Sanjal. When he was some hundred metres away, he stopped, shook the dust off his body, faced his friends and jeered:

"Meet me at the arena tomorrow. I'll finish both of you. You can't compete with me. How will you hold the rope? Ha, ha, ha!" He then disappeared.

The next day hare transformed into the young handsome light-skinned athletic man named Beran Gaye. He went straight to the arena at Sanjal. The spectators, well dressed in traditional costumes were beginning to take their seats which were arranged in a circle. At the right hand corner were drummers with their instruments. The chief's Griot was playing his five-stringed lute called the Halam in Wollof. He was singing about the ancestors of the Sabally family. Beran looked for Hassoum to register his presence and readiness to compete. His presence was acknowledged. Hassoum then enquired:

"Where are your friends, Ali Saine and Katim Njie?"

"I couldn't wait for them. It was getting late so I decided to come. I'm sure they'll soon be here," replied Beran dreading to come face to face with them.

After an hour, Burr Saloum arrived with his entourage. Hassoum quickly went through the names of the ten men who had register for the contest. There were only five men who came. Beran was relieved to hear that Ali Saine and Katim Njie were not participating. He did not know that these two contestants had each strangely transformed themselves into young women. More strangely, they had come with three of their eldest children who also changed into ladies.

The contests started amid drumming. Customarily, the contestants would dance up and down the circle showing physical might before taking a grip of the rope to scare their opponents. The winner of any bout of a tug of war would be escorted by his supporters as they danced round the ring. Beran was strong and skilful. This helped him reach the final round. His animal friends and their children, transformed into ladies were beautiful and well dressed in fitted traditional blouses and loose skirts.

They decided to do their act. Beran approached where the rope lay on the ground, dancing with confidence. The eight women pushed their way to the middle of the ring. Beran turned and saw them. His heart missed a beat. He was afraid that they were elephant, hyena and their children. They were ready to do some mischief. They approached Beran as he picked up the rope in readiness to perform the tug of war. In unison they started to dance kicking up a lot of sand raising blinding dust. Beran got blinded. He closed his eyes as he tried to take a firm grip of the rope. But the signal whistle did not wait. It was blown while he was in this confused state. His opponent took advantage and pulled the rope. Beran fell down.

The winner's supporters rushed into the ring. They picked up their hero and carried him high on their shoulders dancing round the ring. Beran slipped unnoticed and ran away. He immediately transformed to his normal self of a hare and hurried home. He told his family that they must leave immediately. He did not say why. He was certain that elephant, hyena and their children would be in wait for him at the outskirts of **Sanjal.** He was determined not to set eyes on them again. Therefore, he, hare and his family took a southern route and ran towards **Sandu.** Once again he was just too smart for hyena and elephant. Their paths never crossed again. This brought to an end an amicable relationship between three different animals in the area of **Sanjal.**

Two kings make a pact

There were two rulers whose kingdoms were not far from each other. They were named Mansa Musa and Mansa Sumanguru. They were close friends. They were very powerful. They enjoyed a lot of goodwill from their two peoples. They ruled with complete authority. In Mandingo society, the ruler was called Mansa.

The size of each kingdom determined the rank of the Mansa. Between the two rulers, Mansa Musa was the older. His kingdom was extensive. It stretched as far as the eye could see. It was rolling and rich with thick cashew, baobab and mango trees. Groundnut and millet fields rolled hectare after hectare. The vegetation was flourishing green. It was indeed fertile land. Mansa Musa's subjects were hard working. They continuously tilled the land. There was always plenty of food. This kingdom was known as Niamanty.

With much wealth in his possession, Mansa Musa, tall and well built, asserted his nobility through his appearance. He always wore big and well tailored gowns that enhanced his gentility. In addition, he carried the symbol of his royal office, the staff which was made of ebony. It was artistically but meticulously ornamented with unalloyed silver. The head of this regal staff carried a lion's head wearing a golden crown. It was a magnificent symbol of power.

Mansa Musa, in appearance displayed greatness. Most fathers in the rank of nobility could not contain their desire to marry off eligible daughters to him. He had to honour some irresistible moves. He had to be polygamous. He married four wives from the rank of the nobility. They were legal wives. This rooted his reign firmly in the soil of Niamanty.

Mansa Musa contended that these marriages had gracefully satisfied the needs of his reign. He had a passion for beautiful women. Like some of his predecessors, he pursued the urges of his passion. He could add to the number of wives through common law. Common law was more generous since it set no limit to how many. Society though placed such wives at a lower status. However, adherence was diluted with appropriate kindly treatment of such wives and their children.

Over the years, Mansa Musa married three other wives. He loved them all. The three had their living quarters in a separate wing in his palace. His four legal wives shared the same wing. However, conjugal visits were equitably arranged. No wife had a cause against the king. He was much admired as a ruler and a husband. Hidden below his admirable qualities, though laid his weakness of the over powering love for his second common law wife, Musu Kebba. He was incapable of exercising restraint on issues affecting Musu. He loved her. This had to be accepted. It was.

The wives bore him eighteen children, six sons and twelve daughters. The king adored them. He insisted that both sons and daughters receive the upbringing that would prepare them as rulers of the future. The best carers in every sphere of life were engaged.

Mansa Musa's friend, the younger king, Mansa Sumanguru was the ruler of the smaller kingdom of Burawulay. This kingdom was about one hundred kilometres away from Niamanty. Sumanguru was a liberal king. He effectively demonstrated through his policies and their implementation that his primary concern was the welfare of the people. He devolved a lot of authority to the heads of his vassal states of Minkaya and Sankilou for the smooth administration of his kingdom. He believed in delegation so that his representatives would be semi- autonomous and indeed ultimately accountable to him, the supreme king.

Mansa Sumanguru was modest. He was simple in his dress. He was often found wearing a white three piece cotton boubou. In family life, he did not go through the pressure of marrying legal and common law wives as his senior friend. He had four wives. The wives bore him fifteen children: five daughters and ten sons.

Although well respected for his liberalism and modesty, he was secretly criticised for the excessive love demonstrated for his youngest wife, Kaja who was only thirteen years old when they got married. Kaja was in competition with co-wives old enough to be her mother. She had the advantage of young and striking facial features. She was fully aware of her attractive looks. She knew that was strength and therefore availed herself of beauty products and processes. Tattooing of gums and the lower lip was a test of courage and endurance. It was also a source of pride for parents whose daughters go through the process with success. Kaja did.

Kaja's tattooed gums and lip suited her very much. Her teeth sparkled against the indigo blue gums when she smiled broadly. In addition to the remarkable looks were the artistic henna designs covering the palms of her hands and soles of her well shaped feet. Kaja was the embodiment of beauty.

As a very young nursing mother Kaja created a decent way to help her baby boy to feed from her tiny breasts. The child was always pitched on soft pillows to enable him access the breasts with ease during feeding periods. Her ingenuity impressed the king. He allowed her a longer nursing period than usual.

Kaja was very comfortable with all her co-wives. They accepted her warmly. Her age was never an issue. She in turn treated them with respect. She behaved as their younger sister who was always ready to help when asked. This endeared her to them.

The two kings, Sumanguru and Musa maintained a very close relationship. They visited each other frequently and exchanged ideas. They consulted on similar problems to ensure fair settlement of disputes among their peoples. It was during one such visit that both expressed deep concern over the thorny and emotional issue of inheritance and succession. Kingly intervention was not as effective as was desirable. It could not arrest splits within close family members because of conflict of interests. The need to find a method based on social practices was agreed upon. They believed that such a method should keep family members together.

After a lot of hard thinking and debate, the two kings agreed on a system. Sentiments and continuity were the bases of their proposed system. The two royal friends were relieved that they could come up with a means of addressing the thorny issue of inheritance. They feared that when they died, their many wives and children might fall victim to rivalries and family feuds. They therefore made a verbal pact to protect future administrations from such hassles. Each automatically became the carer of the other's household in the event of death. The one who outlived the other would administer the deceased's estates. They ensured that their eldest sons knew about their agreement.

Time was passing by and age was registering its presence on both kings. It was more obvious in the physical structure of the older king. Infections from viruses attacked frequently. Mansa Musa struggled with frequent coughs and pneumonia. The diligent care of the traditional healers brought him temporary relief. He bore his frequent illnesses with indifference. The air of kingly power was ever present. One could say he was defying the weakening effect of poor health on his body. However he recognised that the end was near. He had to be prepared for the inevitable. The pact with his friend, Mansa Sumanguru would see a smooth transfer of power.

Mansa Musa eventually gave in to his illness. He passed away. The news was received with much grief. Sumanguru's household was overcome with sorrow when the emissaries from Niamanty arrived with the sad news. Gloom was like an overhanging cloud in Burawulay. The solemn drum announcing the death of nobility sounded from both palaces. Before long, Mansa Musa's palace was teeming with people. There were intermittent wails and cries as people expressed their feelings at their loss. The crowd was large.

Many messages reached the royal family about kings and nobles who were on their way to the funeral ceremony. Mansa Musa's brothers and the Council decided that the funeral rites would be held five days later. Therefore, the late king would be embalmed to allow all his friends, colleagues and well wishers far and near to attend the funeral rites.

Mansa Sumanguru immediately left for the long and tiring journey on horseback to Niamanty on receiving the death of his friend. He was able to oversee a stately funeral ceremony for his friend. Nobilities of the neighbourhood were able to attend. Clerics prayed for him in a solemn ceremony. Dignitaries spoke well of Mansa

Musa whilst griots narrated the brave deeds and kindness towards his subjects. A beautiful mausoleum well carved in fine stone in the reserved area for royals and nobles received the remains of Mansa Musa.

After the funeral, the palace gradually got deserted. Sumanguru with close family members and friends stayed. Aware that emotions were still high, he decided to allow a long grieving period. The family had to come to terms with the loss before issues of inheritance and succession were examined. In his wisdom and sincerity, Sumanguru suggested that the late king's younger brother should become temporary care of the family. This was well received. With such a stable household, Sumanguru announced his departure.

On horseback and in a depressed mood, Mansa Sumanguru galloped back to Niamanty, five days after the burial of Mansa Musa. He cast his mind back to the events of the few days at his late friend's palace. He shuddered when he relived the treatment of the widows. Discrimination was exercised between the legal and common law wives. Tradition was upheld without restraint by the late king's senior sister. She chose the biggest room, that of the eldest queen to house all the wives as soon as her brother drew his last breath.

The king's sisters came together and decided how to clothe the mourning queens. All four legal wives wore white gowns. The common law wives had to accept dark coloured gowns to mourn their beloved husband. Consideration was not given to the equal treatment they were accorded by their husband.

Sumanguru was relieved that he had no common law wives. He would never be tempted. The shock made him resolve that in the administration of the estate of the late king, dividing the shares would be in accordance with the statutory rules of a patriarch society. The status of wives would be of no consequence. When he arrived home he was given a welcome becoming of a loved king, who was no doubt in mourning.

Days, weeks and months rolled by. Mansa Sumanguru kept an eye on the family of his late friend. Information from reliable sources flowed to him. In this manner, he learnt that his late friend had been succeeded by his younger brother, Bafoday as the king of Niamanty. As he was entitled to marry one of his brother's widows, he made a natural choice. Mansa Bafoday married the late king's second common law wife, Musu Kebba. She became his third wife. The other wives of Mansa Musa remained comfortably in the palace and had their separate living quarters. With tradition fully complied with, it was believed that late Mansa Musa would be in utter peace in his tomb.

The new king was beginning to learn the sweetness of power. He began to be assertive. He secretly decided that the end of mourning was the appropriate time to demonstrate his ability as a capable leader. He, however, waited for six months. Then he summoned his brothers and nephews to talk about how to distribute the properties of his late brother. Dutifully, they all answered to his call. They listened to him with heads bowed low. They all realised that Mansa Bafoday was not aware of the pact entered by their father and Mansa Sumanguru.

The eldest son, Lamin had to reveal the secret to him. He was aware of the need to be tactful. The issue was sensitive. If he had to achieve the desired result he had to be very careful. For Lamin, his late father had always supported his siblings. He was convinced that Mansa Musa entered into the pact to protect his family from being torn apart by discord. The intention was neither to doubt the sincerity nor the capacity of a family member to administer justice in sensitive issues. After listening to his uncle, the new king, Lamin explained calmly:

"There was a day that my father summoned my brother, Dembo and myself in the presence of his friend Mansa Sumanguru of Burawulay. We and the two eldest sons of his friend were also there. My father and his friend told us that they had made an agreement which must be respected by our two families. The pact was that if any of them died, the survivor should be responsible for sharing the assets of the deceased among the dependents. They laid out secretly the way this should be done."

Lamin's siblings nodded in agreement. He was speaking for all of them.

The new king, Bafoday cool and composed after this revelation replied:

"My late brother had made his wishes. They must be respected. Brother Bolong, you will go with our nephews to Mansa Sumanguru of Burawulay. Please extend my greetings and highest regard to him. Assure him that we will respect his decisions on the distribution of the assets of our late brother. Get ready for the journey on horseback to Burawulay. I will direct my travel staff to get the horses ready for you to leave in two days' time."

The royal party consisting of Uncle Bolong and the five sons of late Mansa Musa left on the agreed date just after the first cock crow. It was a glorious morning. The early sun was shining faintly through the horizon. The travellers had their rifles with them for protection. They carried water, Mboudakeh and light cotton clothing for their journey. The group was light hearted and chatty as they took to the roads on the outskirts of small scattered villages. They did not have to stop in those places as they had enough food and water.

On the afternoon of the second day of their journey they came to the first large human settlement. This was the big town of Soorto. It had a population of over one thousand people. Most of the people were traders in cotton and salt. They were very hospitable. The royal party had no problems of refilling their water containers when the need arose. A woman saw them. She graciously invited them to her compound. She gave them water to freshen up. Two big raffia mats with red and green sketches of different birds was spread on the floor of her porch. The men lay on it to take a rest.

The royal party looking for water in Soorto

The woman feasted them with a bowl of steaming rice and meat groundnut stew. She encouraged them to spend a restful night in her house. The hospitality enabled them to renew their journey with relative ease.

Before the sun rose the next morning, the royal party took to the roads again. A whole day of travelling was ahead. Yet they remained alert. As their horses sauntered along, one of late Mansa Musa's sons, Kebba remarked:

"I've seen some hoof prints along the way since mid afternoon. It seems that a camel has used this road recently."

On those words, Ngansu, a brother alighted to have a look. He saw the marks and after examining them he replied:

"That's true. The footprints are still fresh on the ground. The distance between them however tells a story."

Ngansu then sprang up on to his horse and the journey continued all of them remaining quiet. The silence was broken by Kebba on seeing more hoof marks.

"Interesting! This camel has walked a long distance. Here again are its hoof marks. It's curious that each set of the marks display only three legs instead of the normal four. Surely all camels are four-legged. This animal has only three legs."

Ngansu joined in:

"You're very observant, brother Kebba. I did not notice the number of the marks when I examined them."

To their surprise Njogu who was quiet all the way, said:

"Hum. You have failed to make note of the peculiar droppings of the camel. Doesn't that also tell a story about this animal? Such droppings are those of an animal with a short tail."

Feeling weary because of physical exertion and thirst, the royal party decided to take a rest under a huge baobab tree. They had been drinking a lot of water from their water vessels due to the extreme heat. The supply was dwindling. Fortunately the weather started to change. It was getting cool. It would be prudent to save the little water left.

Kebba noticed again fresh hoof marks of the camel. He could not keep quiet. He spoke again.

"That camel we've been talking about must also be one-eyed. Closer looks at the tracks of the hoof marks show it."

"Yes, yes, you are absolutely right" agreed Solo.

Sambujang, another brother added:

"My brother, you've left out an important visible feature. You've all failed to detect the very important weakness of the animal. It is easily frightened. A faint sound without an object sends it dashing away."

While the discussion was on, Uncle Bolong was dozing comfortably under the tree. The group set out again when he woke up. They were all quiet during the best part of this journey. Then they heard a voice. They saw a short and dark skinned man who came to greet them. He told then that his name was Sorrie. He was a hunter living in Burawulay. He boasted that he was the best hunter in the area. He revealed that he kept camels and horses in his compound which was situated not far from the king's palace.

"I know that you are strangers here. But I'm looking for one of my camels. It went astray. Did you come across one on your way?" he enquired. He stammered whenever he opened his mouth.

"Do you mean a three-legged camel?" asked Kebba.

Sorrie explained:

"It's not a three-legged animal. It's a four legged camel. It sustained an injury on the rear left leg. So it limps and avoids using it."

"Oh, I see. That explains why the fourth leg did not make some imprints on the ground," Kebba replied.

He then asked the hunter:

"Does the camel have only one eye?"

"Exactly it does," responded Sorrie with hope in his eyes.

"Does it have a short tail? I'm tempted to believe that the tip of its tail was cut off." Njogu put in.

Before the hunter could make a remark, Sambujang stated in a matter of fact way:

"That camel of yours appears to get easily frightened... Hum! Even the sound from light winds can send it running."

"Hey! You are very right. I cannot tell how easily frightened that camel can get. This is the very reason why it ran away from my compound." Sorrie explained.

"You know a lot about this camel. You cannot deny that you don't have it, you must have my camel. Give it back?" The hunter looked directly into the eyes of Kebba, the first to describe the camel.

"We've neither seen your camel nor have it. We knew what it looked like from its hoof prints," replied Lamin, coming to the defence of his brothers.

"My sons haven't got it. They know about animals. That's all," said Uncle Bolong defensively.

"Oh, I see. So you're defending your young men. Let me tell you one certain thing. In this land there's law. Our king, Mansa Sumanguru is very particular about the rule of law. We'll have to go to him for mediation. I am convinced that you have seen my camel. You must be hiding it. Anyway, the truth will come out. Let's go to the palace. I'll lead the way," replied Sorrie moving eastwards.

"In fact we're on our way to the king. We can all go together. I know that this argument will be over as soon as we meet him," stated Uncle Bolong.

They picked their way through the thin Savannah area of long grasses interspersed with tall rhun palm trees and scattered mango and Solomsolom fruit trees. There was almost no noise. The palace was secretly hidden behind tall shady orange, guava, pawpaw and dittah trees. The drought resistant and medicinal neem tree lined the fence of the palace.

Neem tree

The group walked directly to the palace. Two guards received them at the gate. They ushered them to the king. Uncle Bolong and his nephews paid fitting royal courtesies. Sorrie impatiently started his explanation on the reasons of their presence. He commenced thus:

"Mansa, I've caught the thieves of my camel. Here they're! When I asked them about my camel, they were able to describe it so well."

The king did not recognise his guests. He turned to them and enquired:

"Do you have anything to say? Sorrie said that you have his camel. What does the animal look like?"

Kebba explained:

"We come from Niamanty. On our way here, we saw hoof prints on the ground. As we progressed in our journey, we realised that they were those of a camel that seemed to have three legs. Sorrie in his enquiry revealed that the animal had a wound on one leg. Obviously, it avoided using it when walking. Hence the three foot prints. We were also certain that the animal has only one eye."

"What made you so sure that it is one-eyed?" asked Mansa Sumanguru suddenly getting more interested in what he was hearing.

"I looked at the pattern that it followed when eating. It kept to only one side not both, even though green grass existed on the other side. It confined itself on the side it could see very well because it couldn't see the other side," continued Kebba.

"Who said that the camel gets scared so easily?" the king asked.

"I did," replied Sambujang.

"And why?"

"I came to that conclusion because of its erratic eating pattern. It kept to one side of the area. Then it moved very far to a distant point to resume eating. It seemed that whenever it hears a noise it canters away," explained the brother.

"Oh, I see. Who said that the tip of the camel's tail was cut off?"

"I'm the one. I came to that view after seeing the camel's droppings which are usually solid. In the case of this animal, the droppings were soft and scattered. It is a well known fact that short tail softens the droppings," Njogu explained.

The king felt well informed to give a fair verdict. He addressed Sorrie, the hunter:

"I am convinced that these people have not seen your animal. They've not taken your camel. They are not in possession of it. I therefore order you to go and look for your animal. I and the courtiers absolutely believe that the description of the animal by these men was based on knowledge obtained through care and keep of animals."

Bolong relieved that the ordeal was over with his nephews drew nearer to the king to explain their mission. He introduced his nephews, some of whom Mansa Sumanguru ultimately recognised. They were the sons of his late friend, Mansa Musa of Niamanty. Bolong emotionally stated that the agreement they both entered into was indeed alive. His brother and sitting king was desirous to honour it to the letter. He was therefore asking him to give the matter his urgent attention.

Mansa Sumanguru was touched. The visible signs of emotions, tears rolled down his cheeks. He gave orders for a fitting welcome to be accorded to the royal guests. Immediate arrangements for princely accommodation started. Guest rooms in his private wing were carefully prepared. The head of his kitchen was instructed to slaughter and prepare a goat to be served with the best palm wine ever brewed for dinner. Every instruction was carefully carried out.

A sumptuous feast was served. The guests seemingly enjoyed the food, wine and the lively company. Yet they were perplexed. The king, their host did not head the dinner. A representative deputised for him. He offered no explanation for his master's absence. They as royals did not ask questions. However the treatment was inappropriate. Courteously they made comments on the very tasty food and the wine. Lamin was very impressed with the cooking. This was not endorsed by one of his brother, Dembo who had reservations. He observed:

"The meat has a strange taste. The goat might have been suckled by a dog."

The reaction of the rest of the group was that of dead silence. It was only followed broken by the clattering of glasses as palm wine was being served. Again Lamin could not restrain himself. He struck his tongue against his mouth to show that the drink was too sharp. He pronounced:

"This palm wine must have been tapped from a tree in a graveyard."

These comments though made unintentionally were within the hearing of the king's representative, Karamba. He was shocked. The young men's uncle, Bolong was deeply embarrassed. It had no effect on his nephews. They took no notice. They continued being critical. The king's lack of appearance was a painful issue and an unacceptable flaw in hospitality. To come to terms with it, Dembo examined many reasons and came up with one.

"I can't get this. Our host, the king knows we are full blooded royals. He was the closest friend of a powerful king who fathered us. Why then is he avoiding our presence, courtier? Why is he hiding behind a representative? My answer I would dare to utter. The king feels inadequate before us because he is of mixed breed. He's not as pure as we are. That's it. I'm certain that's correct."

Karamba, the king's representative, overwhelmed with awe, exclaimed:

"Astafurlah!"

He hurriedly left the room to see his master, Mansa Sumanguru. He narrated all that was said.

The king calmly summoned his guests and everyone who partook of the feast. With admirable restraint he addressed the cook:

"My guests enjoyed your tasty food. They however made an observation on the state of your health when you were preparing it. Is it true that you were experiencing your monthly period of menstruation?"

"Your royal highness, it is true. Your orders had to be obeyed. I was identified as the best cook. I couldn't disappoint you," replied the cook.

"Your state of health affected the quality of the juice of the meat which formed the stew. The bread would not soak in the stew. What was more curious was the appearance. Goat meat is lighter than mutton and beef. Fat cover on goat meat is always on the top layer and easily removable. But the one slaughtered in our honour has the fat buried as is usual in dog meat," Lamin joined in.

Mansa Sumanguru was amazed. He asked the cook which goat was slaughtered.

"Your highness, the best in the whole kingdom. Do you remember the goat that lost its mother and was breastfed by the gentlest dog? That was the one I slaughtered for them," she explained proudly.

The king lowered his head because of embarrassment. He then asked whether the best palm wine in the store was provided. The steward who served was eager to be exonerated from blame. He volunteered this information.

"Your royal highness. I got them the best palm wines in the kingdom. The best tapper was ordered to get the special wine from the big palm tree at the edge of the garden. You know that some of its lush branches provide shade to your grandfather's grave. No wine tastes better. The tree is reserved for you and your honoured guests."

"Ha! Wine from a palm tree at the edge of a graveyard! Certainly the feelings we had after drinking were those of sadness rather than high spirits," observed Dembo.

The king morosely shook his head. He was hearing hard facts for the answers he sought to his guests' comments. He felt he had to know the actual reasons for his failed hospitality and being deemed below royalty. It pained him. He had to be bold. He must find out his breed. He addressed this question to his guests:

"And who said that I didn't join you at dinner because I'm not of full royal blood?"

Dembo responded:

"I've my reasons. We're all nobles. Yet you were not comfortable in our company. You promised to share time with us after we had freshened up but you didn't appear. This isn't a kingly act. Instead, you sent us a representative. Young as I am, I know that such

113

behaviour is uncommon in our society. If you doubt my explanation for your unintentional behaviour towards us, I'd advise you to confer with your mum if she's still alive. She's the only one who would tell you the truth about yourself."

The king confidently replied that she was very much alive and ordered that she'd be brought.

Dembo promised to repeat his words in her presence. Indeed he did. The king's mother remained silent for a long time and then explained:

"My son, the young lad is right. Your father was not a good husband. He had too many women in his life. I'd always found him wanting towards my marital rights. As a human being my frailty led me to the arms of a willing and honourable knight. I got pregnant from the amorous meetings. I consequently bore you. I had no regrets for you grew up with the qualities which the king couldn't find in the sons he thought he fathered."

The king was mute for a long time. He finally found his voice and courage and said:

"You have adequately demonstrated that you have the capacity to take care of my late friend, your father's affairs. I'm particularly encouraged by the thought and consideration that went into the selection of this delegation. The wives are adequately represented by all the sons of my deceased friend. No one can determine whether you share the same mother or not. The relationship between the brothers shows that the closely knit family is being nurtured. If we all have such children and brothers, we'll be at peace with ourselves.

We'll be confident that when we're no longer around, the family will not disintegrate.

I must be honest enough to acknowledge that I lack the wisdom and stature to fulfil the duty imposed on me by my agreement with my late friend. I therefore vacate my responsibility and entrust it in your capable hands. I am confident you'll carry out the duty judiciously."

The group from Niamanty was humbled. They insisted that the pact must be respected. Mansa Sumanguru assured them of his confidence in the fair administration of the estate of the late king. He proposed that he would intervene if their decisions were rejected by any member of the family. With this understanding, Mansa Musa's family returned home. The new ruler of Niamanty, Mansa Bafoday together with his brothers and nephews agreed that the overriding consideration should be to protect the interest of late Mansa Musa's children. He had treated all of them in the same manner. Therefore they would receive equal entitlement as boys. The girls will get the same portion in the assets.

The wives would continue to live in the palace. They would enjoy all the privileges as during the reign of their deceased husband. Peace reigned in Mansa Bafoday's palace.

Hare and hyena pay a visit to the king

Hare and hyena had been close friends and very good neighbours since they set up their homes near each other in the forest of Tanala. This area was covered with a vegetation of dwarf grasses and shrubs intertwining with different fruit trees, rhun palm, palm kernel and Moringa trees. They would go out in search of food together or when not so engaged they would sit under a big Netteh fruit tree to enjoy some shade and also chat on issues of the moment. One such day, they were discussing some of their dreams when they realised that they both wanted to visit the palace of the king of Sukardeboh. They had heard so much about the magnificent palace, the splendour and the many domestic animals owned by the royal family. They thought that they deserved to take a break and be exposed to what was special there. They started to plan a journey to the palace and discussed the presents they could take along.

They agreed that the presents should be things unique. They would have to obtain them in their own environment. Hare as the smart partner proposed:

"We'll have to go two different ways to succeed. You can take the road to the left and I'll go right. We'll each go in search of the best present. If possible, let's get back before sunset. Then we'll compare. However, we will each keep what we have found and that would be presented to the king."

"Oh, do you think I'm a fool. Why should I take the road to the left? Nobody eats with a left hand. I'll take the road to the right because I'm sure I'll get food which will be presentable to a king. I can even have some of what I have found for myself. I don't intend to cover a long distance to the palace on an empty stomach. Besides, if I'm a bit full, I won't desire for a while and this would get the king irritated. So you take the road to the left and I'll take the opposite way" emphasized hyena.

"There's no need to argue on this. I'll go whichever way you propose," replied hare.

Hyena took the road to the right whilst hare went left. They each walked very far before seeing anything worthy of consideration. Tired and feeling very hot, hare saw a distance away, a big Detah tree with its many branches giving shady covering in a wide circle beneath it. Hare hurried there to take a rest in its shade. He chose a spot covered with thick tuft of green grass. He looked around to check for small ants that could disturb him as he was going to take a nap.

Hare sat down. On looking at the tree trunk he saw some large ants moving towards the opposite side of the tree. Curiosity made him get up to find out what these ants were following.

"What am I seeing? I can't believe my eyes! Is this a mouth or a hole? Wonders will never cease. I have to see what is inside."

Hare tiptoed towards the hole. He was unable to see anything. He was not tall enough. Interest had got the better hold of him.

"I hate being too short. If only this tree can be made to become shorter, I'll satisfy myself by getting into that hole to see what is inside," hare said wishfully.

A wishful thinking sudden turned into a command. The tree started to reduce its height. Gradually, it continued to become low until it reached the level of hare's chest. Hare became afraid. He trembled like a leaf. He asked himself how a tree could obey him.

Hare looked around. He saw no one. Timidly, he cautiously went nearer and peered in the hole. He did not go far enough. He then summoned courage and put his head a bit further into the hole. He was confounded. He then put his right hand into the hole to touch what he saw. Satisfying the urge to find out what he had touched, he brought out a piece of a soft tissue which turned out to be a dripping honeycomb.

In an exhilarating tone, hare exclaimed:

"Hey! What a luck and find! This is something I can munch whilst resting. I must savour this".

On finishing the piece after many lickings hare went again and got some more. He could not stop and ate until he was full. He then laid in front of the hole of the tree to rest. He slept for two hours. He woke up with a start when he saw the sun fading in the horizon. He remembered he was to meet hyena before sunset at the same crossroads they parted. He had to hurry up before he was late. He took out his bag and filled it with honey. He licked some more before rushing back to his appointment with hyena.

Hyena was on time waiting for his friend. As soon as he saw him, he called out:

"Come my little friend. I have a lot of goodies for the king. I'll not tell you what I have. Come and take a look."

Hyena opened his bag. As soon as he did beetles, butterflies, lizards and locusts jumped out of the mouth of the bag.

"Help! Help! Help!" Hyena cried out to his friend. They must capture them. A hot chase followed. They succeeded to catch one of each of the goodies hyena had earlier. He was upset because his bag became light as a result of the loss.

"Let me see what you've got, hare," he asked of his friend.

"Nothing much," replied hare opening his bag a little for hyena to peep through.

"What you have is dark and sticky. What's it?" He questioned.

"As I said earlier, it's nothing much. I got a wee bit of honey for the king," hare explained carefully.

"Can I have a taste? You know some honey is nicer than others. I have very good taste buds. I can tell you whether you have the good type if you allow me to have some," hyena coaxed his friend.

Hare smartly made a small opening to allow hyena's thumb in so that he could only get enough to cover it. Hyena dipped his big finger in the bag, carefully got it out and then licked it. He liked the taste and begged for more.

"Oh no! I can't let you have all. We had agreed earlier that each of us should keep his own. Why are you now trying to change what was agreed upon?" asked hare securing his bag tightly to his chest as he stood on his hind legs.

That's true, but just a little. Please, please, please," pleaded hyena.

Hare, knowing better, put his own small finger in the bag got it covered with the honey and gave it to hyena to lick. Hyena wickedly held onto the finger and wouldn't let it go.

Suffering from much pain, hare pleaded for the release of his finger.

"Your finger will not be freed until you show me the tree where the honey is," stated hyena.

Unable to bear the pain and afraid to lose his finger, hare led hyena to the place. He took his friend to the location of the tree and explained how to get it to a suitable height for him to access the honey.

"Demonstrate how it is done," hyena commanded hare as they got nearer the Detah tree.

Hare had to do what he was told. With the magical words, he said:

"I wish this tree can become as short as me."

The tree obeyed instantly and started to lower down. Hyena immediately released hare's finger in haste to act. He ran to the tree and put his head in the hole of the trunk and ravenously licked honey until he had his fill. Then he grabbed his bag and emptied it of the beetle, lizard and locust in order to fill it with honey. He secretly vowed to take more than hare. He therefore convinced him that they should delay their journey to the king's palace to the next day. Hare agreed.

The following day the two friends set out early. They walked through the dry grassy area of Kerr Pateh. As they went further they entered thicker vegetation which had Netteh, palm kernel, mango, coconut and palm trees intermingling with tall green grasses. Hyena said that he wanted to take a break. He must fulfil nature's urge. He handed over his bag to his friend.

Walking just some fifteen metres away, hyena was about to ease himself when hare called out to him:

"What are you trying to do there? That's the property of the king's sister. If you don't care for a warm reception at the palace, I do. Don't be so reckless. This is royal property. Don't abuse it. Move further," advised hare.

"How did you know that this is royal property?" enquired hyena.

"I was taking a walk the other day and saw some men clearing it. I overheard one of them saying that the king's sister intended to use it as a coos farm next rainy season," explained hare.

"Thank you. You are right. I should go in further then," said hyena.

He took more than fifteen steps away before starting to settle down with nature.

"Not there too! That's the land of the king's aunt," warned hare.

Hyena got suspicious and wondered. What does my tricky friend want? I hope he doesn't have some sinister plans. But then he has a bag of honey just as mine. He can't change that. I'll do as he says and avoid royal property, mused hyena.

He took a long, threatening look at hare and then went out of his sight.

Hare was in a hurry for this opportunity. He emptied the honey in hyena's bag to fill his own. Then he went ahead to fill up his friend's bag with stools up to half way. Then he filled the rest of it with honey to conceal the obnoxious part. Satisfied with what he did, he quickly tied the two bags with strings.

Ten minutes later, hyena emerged confronting his friend with these words:

"What did you do to my bag? It was not tied this way. The knot tied was a bit loose. I set a trap for you. I know you are fond of cheating or playing dirty tricks on your friends. So you walked into the trap."

Unaffected by his friend's remarks, hare challenged:

"Check your bag and see if I took anything. I tied mine and decided to do the same for you. If I did not, you would have accused me of being selfish. Now instead of appreciation, I'm being rewarded by suspicion from my dear friend."

Hyena dismissed the comments because he did not believe hare but moreover he wasn't ready to have exchanges with him. He opened his bag, saw the honey on the top and then drew the string tightly.

"Let's go. We must enter the palace before nightfall," hyena addressed his friend as they picked their way and passed through Sare Molloh. They succeeded to enter the seat of the king, Sukardeboh just after dusk. The guests were received and ushered into the courtyard.

The king gave them audience an hour later. It was usual for subjects to travel from far places to visit their king. Thus it was not a surprise to learn of the visit of hyena and hare.

With bags in hand they spoke in turns:

"Our dear king! We are here to pay our respects to you and your family. We want you to graciously accept these modest presents from us. We pray that you'll find them as a fitting gift," said hare as he presented him with his bag of honey.

Hyena stood up, he was not to be out done. He added:

"We have long planned this visit. We thought it important to bring unique presents for our dear ruler. As soon as we succeeded we set out on this journey. This too is my present to you. A taste of it, dear king will give you the sweetest taste!"

The king opened the two bags which were side by side. He dipped his finger in the first bag and licked it. It tasted very good.

"Where did you get this delicious honey from? I've never tasted such a high quality of honey before. Now, let me have a go at the contents of the second bag."

This time the king being confident that the contents would be good put his hand into the bag up to his elbow. He pulled back his hand holding soft balls which carried a foul smell. With great disappointment and horror, he turned and looked at hyena. He called his wife for some soap and water. He washed his hand and then addressed his guests:

"I don't understand how this could happen. The first bag was full of pure delicious honey. The second bag which was given to me by hyena has a foul smell. It is dishonour against a royal person. Why should this happen?"

"I'm ashamed. I took good care of my bag and its contents until I found it necessary to entrust it to my friend, hare. He must have tampered with my bag during my brief absence. I deeply regret this painful incident," responded hyena unable to look the king in his eyes.

The guests spent two uneventful days at the palace. In the evening of the third day, the king gave them audience in his chambers. He instructed Chana, the chief of household thus:

"Take my guests to the cattle shed. Allow them to look around. Let each choose any rope that is a tether. They can take their choice and bring them to me."

"My great king, the herd is grazing and will not be back until dusk. There is nothing in the shed at the moment," said Chana.

"I have given you my instructions. Lead them there," commanded the king.

Chana led the guests to the shed. Hare and hyena went from one post to the other inspecting the ropes used to tether the cattle. Neither of them could make up their minds. After going round the shed thrice, hyena picked a big expensive looking rope. Hare selected an old nylon one. They then returned to the king in the palace.

At nightfall, the king directed Chana to return to the herd with the two guests. They should each take the animal whose rope they held. Hyena felt that the size and quality of his rope would earn him the biggest bull in the shed.

On arrival at the shed, they found that all the cattle had returned. With the ropes in hand, the herdsman looked at each and guided them to the animals. Hyena was shocked. His rope was tied to a frail and hungry looking bull. That was his luck. He guided the animal away with his head bent and his tail held between his rear legs. He was mortified. He could not bear to exchange glances with hare. The rope that his friend chose belonged to a healthy looking white cow with beautifully curved horns.

Chana told the two friends, hyena and hare that the king had given them the cattle as gifts. They were to spend the night in the palace. They would leave the next day.

The two friends after a night's rest started their journey early the next morning. They allowed their animals to graze intermittently along the way so that they would arrive home at dusk. In their discussions, they amicably agreed to take turns to tend the cattle. Deep down in his mind, hyena wanted an opportune time to retaliate hare's deeds.

The journey back proceeded slowly for it seemed that hare's cow was pregnant. A few weeks after their return home, the cow gave birth. It happened at a time hyena had taken them out to graze. Hyena took care of the birth process. He gathered the umbilical cord and kept it in his bag. He decided that he was going to take the new born calf for himself. He headed with the cattle for home.

When they were near, hyena separated the calf from its mother. He took the umbilical cord and forced it into the bottom of his bull. The calf and her mother mooed sorrowfully. When hyena saw hare he tried to explain:

"My bull has given birth to a bouncing calf. Isn't it beautiful?"

"When did bulls start giving birth? This is not your calf. It's mine. The cow that the king gave me was heavily pregnant," challenged hare.

They had hot exchanges. None of them would accept fault. In the end they decided to go to the king for arbitration. They did. When the matter was explained to him, the king rose and said:

"Just give me a few minutes. I have to attend to the needs of my elderly uncle. He's just had a baby. We've got to arrange the naming ceremony."

"He's a man. How can he have a child?" asked hyena.

"Exactly! It's the same as what you are claiming. How can a bull have a calf? Give the calf back to the rightful owner," replied the king.

The dispute was then resolved and the two friends resumed their shared responsibility of tending their herd. With time, the herd multiplied. Greed however soon got hold of hare. He thought of ways to take over complete ownership of the whole herd. He came up with the idea of looking very attractive. He therefore got his upper and lower gums deeply tattooed. They looked beautiful. He then went in search of hyena in the open areas. He was lucky to find him outside Kerr Pateh.

"Hi, my friend. I'm a bit lonely and I missed your company so I thought of not only surprising you but to join you here," said hare with a wide smile which showed his tattoo gums.

"What a pleasant surprise! You look beautiful when you smile. What have you done to your gums?" asked hyena.

"Oh, you mean the tattoo. My aunt did it for me. Have you met her before? They say I'm a carbon copy of her," explained hare.

"Please tell me where I can find her. I'm interested in tattooing my upper gums."

"Okay. You always pass by her sitting under that palm kernel tree in the middle of the forest of Tanala. She's usually there in mid afternoon wearing a wrapper round her waist just like those young girls who do their laundry by the river. You can't miss her. If you wish I'll tell her about your desire to be tattooed. She'll willingly do it," said hare.

The following day was hare's turn to tend the cattle. He quickly took them to an open area with some fodder and then returned to sit under the palm kernel tree. He must look like his aunt. His dress had to be similar. He put on a cotton wrapper round his waist. By his side, he had a piece of cloth on which were the seven thorns sharper than fine needles. Beside the cloth was a cup full of burnt groundnut oil.

Hyena came to the tree and was surprised when he was close.

"Is this not hare? I saw you with the herd a few minutes ago. Have you left them on their own?"

"You are mistaken. I'm not your friend, hare. I'm his aunt. We look very much alike," was the answer.

"You are my friend, hare. I'm not convinced. The similarity is unbelievable. I'll have to check on his whereabouts. Wait here. I'm going to check whether he's tending our herd," stated sceptical hyena.

Hyena left to go and look for his friend. Hare seized the opportunity to baffle hyena. He hurried towards the shorter route to get to where he left the cattle grazing. He got there ahead of hyena who on arrival was surprised to see hare.

"Well, well. I'm from your aunt. I can't believe that you two could look so much alike. I came to check that you were here. Since I've seen you, I'm going back for the tattoo," explained hyena.

Reassured, hyena left. When he was out of sight, hare repeated his feat. He left by the shortest route to ensure that he would be under the tree before hyena arrived.

"I'm still puzzled by the similar features between you, the aunt and my friend hare. Somehow I feel the similarity is not natural. Something is wrong but I can't put my finger on it. I'll go again and check whether he's where I left him," said the puzzled hyena.

He went and again found his friend was there taking care of the herd. After three repeated checking journeys to the place where the cattle were grazing, hyena finally resigned to go ahead with the tattoo.

"I now believe you're hare's aunt. I have said to your nephew that I want to have my upper gum tattooed. Will you do it for me?" he asked.

"Of course. You're my nephew's closest friend. I'll gladly do it for you."

Hare coughed up a new trick. Instead of using the thorns to carry out the pricking, hare buried each of them deep into hyena's gums. He then rubbed the oil on hyena's gums and told him he had carried out the process successfully. Hyena went straight to the ground where he had left his friend and addressed him:

"I'm deeply grateful to your aunt. She's done the tattoo for me. But you never told me that the process was so painful. My gums are sore. I can barely move them."

"Don't worry. It will heal very soon. Then you'll forget about the pain," coaxed hare.

This was not so. Hyena's gums got swollen over the next few days. He could neither eat nor sleep. He returned to his friend to complain:

"I still have no relief. Your aunt did a bad job for me. My gum is swollen and I can't sleep."

Hare looked away for a second. It was a trick again to let the comments pass.

"Interesting! Hey, hyena look! That's a squirrel! Catch it before it escapes," said hare.

"Where is it?" asked greedy hyena turning to follow hare's gaze.

Hyena madly dashed towards the spot he saw the squirrel. The rodent bolted and circled the trees many times. When it saw a hole near a fallen tree, it went for it. In his high speed, hyena accidentally knocked his head on the remaining trunk of the tree. He sustained serious injuries. He bled to death. Hare succeeded in his tricks to capture control and ownership of the joint herd of cattle.

GLOSSARY

- **Amulet** - talisman, charm.

- **Bankanas** – this is called Mankanaso in Mandingo. It is a shrub with medicinal value. The leaves can either be boiled or soaked in water. The water can be used to treat eye infection. 1999).

- **Bolong** - local name for tributary.

- **Chereh** - pounded coos kneaded into small grains and then steamed. It can be eaten with stew. It can also be a light meal when eaten with milk and sugar.

- Detah - this is a green fruit. The fresh ripe fruit is eaten raw. It is known as Tallo in Mandingo. The scientific name is Detarium Senegalensis.

- **Leveret** - young hare.

- **Mboudakeh** - steamed coos cereal called chereh mixed with sugar and peanut butter

- Moringa - the Wollof calls it Nebedie. It is known as Nedebayo in Mandingo and Ndbeday in Pulaar. The leaves of the Moringa are cooked as soup. The young leaves and fruit are prepared as vegetable.

- **Netteh** - this is called Neto in Mandingo. The ripe fruit can be eaten. It can also be dried and then pounded into flour. The pulp can be soaked in water, and salt or sugar added to it. It is a nice drink.

- **Neem tree** - this is a medicinal plant whose leaves are boiled and the solution drank for the cure of malaria. It has other curing properties.

- **Njarr** - creamy sour milk shake. It is used as a desert.

- **Ritti** - a lute played by Fula, Serere and Wollof musicians.

- **Sepah** - roots put in water cooler to give good and satisfying taste to the water. These roots have medicinal values for the stomach.

- **Shillings** - this is the currency used during the colonial period for The Gambia, Sierra Leone, Ghana and Nigeria.

- **Solom solom** - the mature ripe fruits are eaten raw. The young fresh leaves are chewed. The fruit is called Kosito in Mandingo.

- **Timing timingo** - this is a small plant that is dried and put in many magical potents.

- **Zimba** -masquerade of Wollof tribe.

www.ingramcontent.com/pod-product-compliance
Lightning Source LLC
Chambersburg PA
CBHW030335270326
41926CB00010B/1640